Don't Date

Have a Relationship Instead

Hani Iskander

**KNOWLEDGE
PUBLISHING**

**KNOWLEDGE
PUBLISHING**

Published by Knowledge Publishing,
a business of Cube Capital Pty Ltd

ISBN: 978-0-9756642-3-0

DEDICATION

To those searching for genuine love in this modern age.

One single swipe promises endless horizons: instant connections, abundant choices, and a spark of finding "the one."

Yet, for so many, that promise dissolves into an illusion. Hours spent on scrolling profiles, stumbling through aimless chats, and enduring dates that ignite hope but yield disappointment.

If you feel frustrated and wonder why finding someone who truly understands you is challenging, you're not alone.

This book is for you.

It's time to quit chasing fleeting ties and focus on building something real.

Within these pages, you'll discover more than advice; you'll find a roadmap—a guide to genuinely forging the lasting bond you crave.

This book is your lifeline—an invitation to seize control, cut through the noise, and ultimately find authentic, lasting love.

Here's to love—enduring and yours for the making.

NOTE FROM THE AUTHOR

Dear friends

If these words find you, you've already embarked on a bold expedition that winds through digital swipes, first encounters, and the deeper waters of genuine connection.

Don't Date! pulls back the curtain on modern romance and offers practical insights for navigating this ever-shifting terrain. Here's a quick glimpse of what awaits:

Chapter 1: Decoding Digital Courtship: Your profile isn't just text and photos—it's a window into who you are. Learn to paint a genuine online presence that sparks real interest.

Chapter 2: Beyond the Screen. Making the First Move: Step from the virtual world to face-to-face reality with timing and authenticity, the hallmarks of every meaningful connection.

Chapter 3: The First Date. Setting the Stage for Success: Arrive prepared, stay true to yourself, and see this as mutual discovery rather than an evaluation.

Chapter 4: Reading Between the Lines. Understanding Nonverbal Cues: Body language speaks volumes where words fail. Tune in to the subtle signals that reveal true intentions.

Chapter 5: Communication is Key. Building a Connection: Balance your story with your partner's.

Authentic connection thrives on shared listening and openness.

Chapter 6: The Follow-Up. Post-First Date Etiquette: Stay mindful of interest levels and compatibility. The follow-up is the bridge to either possibility or closure.

Chapter 7: Handling Rejection and Disappointment: Not every "hello" leads to "happily ever after." Embrace setbacks as lessons that refine your path forward.

Chapter 8: The Second Date and Beyond. Deepening the Connection: Bring creativity and vulnerability to each encounter. Let curiosity guide you toward greater intimacy.

Chapter 9: From Casual to Serious. The Transition Phase: When it's time to pivot from "me" to "we," clarity and candid communication can make all the difference.

Chapter 10: Maintaining a Healthy Relationship: Balance independence with togetherness and allow your bond to evolve with every season of life.

Chapter 11: Long-Term Commitment. Making It Last: Build a future grounded in trust, shared values, and unwavering commitment.

Remember, this journey isn't just about finding someone— it's about discovering yourself along the way. May ***Don't Date!*** be your compass to lasting love as you forge the connection you've been seeking.

Stay curious, keep the faith and let love lead. Your story's still unfolding.

CONTENTS

CONTENTS

ACKNOWLEDGMENTS

Like so many others, I've navigated the unpredictable waters of dating. I've seen tens upon tens of friends and acquaintances traverse their own routes—some wading gingerly, others diving headfirst. Each believed they'd found "the one," yet it didn't last for many. Inevitably, they were left asking: What am I doing wrong? Why do others seem so lucky?

What struck me wasn't the uniqueness of each story—though every relationship feels singular at first—but the surprising consistency when they unravelled. Patterns emerged, common threads linking struggles, triumphs, and heartbreaks. For all the ways we think our experiences are singular, they often aren't. The same questions, missteps, and frustrations resurface time and again.

This book would not exist without my close and distant friends who have braved the dating pool and trusted me with their stories. They shared excitement, hope, disappointment, and doubt. Through their honesty and vulnerability, a clearer picture formed—not just of what goes wrong but of what could go right.

Thank you to those friends and countless others who shared their perspectives. Your courage to reflect, generosity, and vulnerability provided the foundation for this book.

This book is as much yours as it is mine.

ACKNOWLEDGMENTS

Chapter 1

Decoding the Digital Courtship

Part 1

The Psychology Behind Online Profiles

"We are what we pretend to be, so we must be careful about what we pretend to be."

– Kurt Vonnegut

Understanding the psychology behind online profiles becomes crucial in a world where first impressions are often made through a screen. These profiles are not mere collections of photos and text; they are windows into our desires, fears, and hidden truths.

Crafting Identities

Online profiles in dating apps are akin to personal billboards. They are crafted, often meticulously, to project a certain image. Here, we delve into the psychology of self-presentation. Why do we choose certain photographs over others? What do our word choices in bios say about us? This exploration would reveal how these choices reflect broader social trends and individual psychologies.

Consider the photograph: a smiling face, a group of friends, a moment captured in a foreign land. Each image tells a story of who we are and who we want to be seen as. The profile picture is the first handshake and eye contact in this digital courtship. It's a carefully curated introduction, often designed to project confidence, attractiveness, and even status.

ooo

Jake and Melissa connected on a dating app, drawn together by their engaging profiles. Jake's profile featured a photo of him at a volunteer event, smiling broadly as he helped construct a community garden. His bio was a mix of humor and sincerity, mentioning his passion for environmental causes and his love for indie music. Melissa's profile showcased her adventurous spirit with a photo of her mountain climbing in Peru. Her bio was a witty blend of her travel interests, cooking exotic cuisines, and yoga.

When they met for coffee, both were pleasantly surprised. Jake admired Melissa's genuine passion for adventure, which extended beyond her online persona. For Melissa, Jake's commitment to community service wasn't just for show – it was a significant part of his life. This initial meeting illuminated how their online identities, while carefully curated, were rooted in their true selves, reflecting their values and aspirations. Their profiles weren't just self-presentations; they were gateways to deeper, authentic connections.

ooo

The Language of Self-Description

Moving beyond the visual, we enter the realm of text – the bios and descriptions. Here, every word counts. The language used in these descriptions is a dance of self-promotion and vulnerability. Users often straddle the line between presenting their best selves and maintaining authenticity. It's a modern-day version of the age-old question: How do we present ourselves to a potential partner?

The language of online profiles often mirrors societal norms and expectations. For example, the prevalence of phrases like "adventurous," "loves to travel," or "foodie" does not just refer to personal interests but also speaks to broader cultural values of exploration, curiosity, and indulgence.

ooo

Elena, an architect with a penchant for poetry, crafted her dating profile with a careful balance of charm and depth. Her bio read, "Designing buildings by day, weaving words by night. In love with the city lights and countryside retreats." This mix of professionalism and personal passion intrigued Sam, an urban planner and amateur guitarist, whose own profile echoed a similar harmony: "Shaping cities, strumming melodies. Seeking shared rhythms in life's vast symphony."

When they chatted online, they quickly discovered a mutual appreciation for the arts and urban aesthetics. Their conversation seamlessly moved from discussing their favorite architectural marvels to exchanging lines from their favorite poets. Both used their bios to list interests and express an intersection of their professional and personal worlds.

Their profiles, a blend of self-promotion and authenticity, were like open doors to their personalities, inviting someone to understand what they did and who they were. This nuanced self-description went beyond the superficial, fostering a connection based on shared values and deeper interests.

ooo

The Unspoken Truths

But what lies beneath these polished exteriors? A deeper look would prompt us to understand the unspoken truths hidden in these profiles. The omission of certain information, the ambiguity in a description, the choice of a specific quote – these subtleties can offer glimpses into a person's true self, insecurities, and desires.

In this digital courtship, profiles are more than just a means to an end. They are reflections of our individual and collective psychologies – a tapestry of desires, fears, and identities playing out in the digital arena. Understanding this psychology is the first step in decoding the complex dance of digital dating.

ooo

Amanda's profile on the dating app showed poise and cheerfulness. It included photos of her at various social events, always surrounded by friends. Her bio was upbeat and filled with emojis, and it discussed her love for travel and social gatherings. However, it omitted any mention of her quieter side, her passion for reading, and her evenings spent painting.

When she matched with Alex, whose profile was an array of adventurous photos and witty one-liners, their initial conversations revolved around their shared love for travel and bustling social life. However, as they continued to chat, Alex noticed the nuances in Amanda's messages – references to a quiet weekend reading, a subtle hint of her artistic side. This prompted him to share his less visible interest in gardening and writing.

Their connection deepened as they uncovered these unspoken truths about each other. While true to a part of her personality, Amanda's profile had masked her more introspective side, just as Alex's profile had hidden his quieter passions. In this digital dance, they discovered that profiles are a surface-level introduction, and the real connection begins when the unspoken truths are shared, revealing a complete picture of their personalities.

Part 2

The Art of Making the Right Swipe: Selecting Potential Partners

"Love does not consist of gazing at each other,
but in looking outward together in the same direction."

– Antoine de Saint-Exupéry

Moving forward, we will turn our attention to the intricate process of finding a suitable match in digital dating. This pursuit calls for a delicate balance of instinct and deliberation, much like the subtle choices we make in our daily routines.

The Strategy Behind the Swipe

Swiping right or left may seem simple, yet it involves a complex web of psychological and social factors. We delve into what influences these split-second decisions. Is it purely physical attraction, or are there other, more nuanced factors at play?

Consider the composition of the profile picture, the subject's expression, and the background. Research indicates that certain elements can elicit a more positive response—a genuine smile, a hint of mystery, or a snapshot that narrates a story. Similarly, the content of the bio can sway decisions. A witty, well-crafted bio might capture interest, while clichés may lead to a quick dismissal.

The Psychology of Choice

The psychology of choice in this scenario is fascinating. Our swiping patterns can reveal much about our preferences, biases, and fears. Our personal histories, cultural backgrounds, and the intricate workings of the human psyche deeply influence these fleeting choices.

For example, the inclination to swipe right on profiles that seem familiar or safe versus those that offer something new and challenging can shed light on our relationship approach. Do we embrace risk or gravitate toward the comfort of the familiar? These choices reflect our broader attitudes toward love and life.

The Illusion of Abundance

The 'paradox of choice' concept becomes particularly relevant in online dating. With an abundance of options, choosing can become overwhelming, potentially leading to less satisfaction. This paradox highlights how an excess of choices can often leave us haunted by the possibilities of missed opportunities and better options that might be just a swipe away.

Understanding these aspects of digital dating selection helps us navigate the complexities of online matchmaking and provides insights into our behaviour and preferences for pursuing meaningful connections.

Understanding this dynamic is crucial in selecting potential partners. It's about recognising that while the digital world offers a vast sea of options, the quality of connections matters more than the quantity.

Moving Beyond the Swipe

Finally, we consider the transition from swiping to genuine connection. How do we move beyond the superficiality of profiles and photos to forge real, meaningful connections? This step requires moving from the realm of speculation into the world of action – initiating conversation, finding common ground, and exploring the potential for a deeper connection.

When making the right swipe, the goal is not just to find a match but to embark on a journey that could lead to a meaningful, lasting relationship. This process combines intuition, an understanding of human psychology, and a willingness to look beyond the surface.

Do's and Don'ts

Do's:

1. **Be Thoughtful in Profile Creation:** Reflect your true self in your profile, balancing honesty with the desire to make a good first impression.

2. **Look for Depth in Profiles:** Seek profiles showing depth and authenticity beyond attractive photos.

3. **Pay Attention to Details:** Notice the subtle cues in profiles and messages that reveal more about a person's character and interests.

4. **Be Open to Surprises:** Connect with people who might not fit your usual 'type' but could offer a refreshing perspective.

5. **Initiate Meaningful Conversations:** Move beyond superficial topics to engage in conversations that reveal shared values and interests.

Don'ts:

1. **Don't Judge Solely on Appearance:** Avoid making snap judgments based solely on profile pictures.

2. **Avoid Clichés in Your Profile:** Avoid overused phrases and generic descriptions that don't convey your unique personality.

3. **Don't Ignore Red Flags:** Be cautious of profiles that seem too perfect or inconsistent.

4. **Don't Get Overwhelmed by Choices:** Avoid the paradox of choice by focusing on quality over quantity in your matches.

5. **Don't Hesitate to Move Beyond the App:** Don't hesitate to suggest meeting in person when you feel a genuine connection.

Chapter 2

Beyond the Screen
- Making the First Move

Part 1

Crafting Engaging Conversations Online

*"The single biggest problem in communication
is the illusion that it has taken place."*

– George Bernard Shaw

Turning our attention to dialogue, we explore the nuanced craft of initiating and maintaining engaging online conversations. This is critical to breaking through the surface-level nature of photos and profiles. Like a refined social dance, this stage calls for a precise blend of sincerity, tact, and timely interaction.

The Art of the Opening Message

The opening message in an online dating relationship is like the first moves in a chess game—strategic, thoughtful, and often indicative of the interaction's trajectory. Like first impressions in any social interaction, the key is to be intriguing yet genuine, balancing showing interest without seeming overbearing.

What makes an opening message compelling? Often, it's the ability to connect over a shared interest, a humorous observation, or a thought-provoking question. Crafting a personal message, showing that you've engaged with the profile rather than merely glanced at photos, initiates a dialogue that encourages a response and paves the way for organic conversation growth.

ooo

After scrolling through numerous profiles, Daniel was captivated by Maria's, adorned with quotes from classic literature and photos from her travels to historic sites. Her bio mentioned her love for historical novels and Renaissance art, sparking an idea in Daniel's mind. He crafted his opening message carefully: "I couldn't help but notice your quote from 'Pride and Prejudice.' Elizabeth Bennet's wit is unparalleled. By the way, that photo of you at the Uffizi Gallery made me reminisce about my last visit there. Do you have a favorite Renaissance artist?"

Impressed by Daniel's attention to detail and shared interest, Maria felt a surge of excitement. His message was not just a generic greeting but a personalised connection to her interests, sparking a natural flow of conversation. She replied enthusiastically, discussing her love for Botticelli, which soon branched into various topics of mutual interest.

Daniel's opening message had set the tone for their interaction: thoughtful, engaging, and genuinely interested in who Maria was beyond her profile pictures. It started a conversation that felt less like a chess game and more like a seamless dance of mutual discovery.

ooo

The Dynamics of Digital Conversation

Once the conversation begins, the challenge is to keep it flowing smoothly. Finding a rhythm in online conversation, a balance of give and take, is crucial for engagement. This means being responsive yet not overbearing, open but not oversharing, and inquisitive without being intrusive.

An important aspect is the ability to read and respond to the conversation's tone and direction. Online interactions require a nuanced understanding of language and emotion. Emojis, punctuation, and the timing of responses are significant in conveying mood and intention.

ooo

Emily and Mark had matched on a dating app, and their initial exchanges were promising. Mark's first message about their mutual love for hiking had sparked an easy back-and-forth. As they continued to chat, Emily carefully maintained a balanced conversation. She shared stories about her favorite trails and asked Mark about his hiking experiences, keeping the dialogue interactive and engaging.

Mark appreciated how Emily used emojis to add warmth to her messages, and her well-timed responses kept the conversation lively. He was also mindful of not dominating the chat. When discussing a recent hiking trip, he included questions about Emily's adventures, showing genuine interest in her experiences.

The way they communicated was a dance of sorts—a harmonious exchange in which neither overshadowed the other. Emily's use of occasional humor and thoughtful questions, combined with Mark's attentive and engaging replies, created a comfortable rhythm. They were able to read each other's tone, even in a digital space, and adjust their messages accordingly. Their conversation flowed naturally, without feeling pressured or overlooked, illustrating the art of maintaining a dynamic and enjoyable digital dialogue.

ooo

Authenticity and Vulnerability

Authenticity and vulnerability are potent tools in online dating. Demonstrating vulnerability in digital conversations can foster a deeper connection. This involves sharing personal stories, revealing genuine interests, and being open about one's thoughts and feelings.

However, this vulnerability must be balanced with discretion and safety. Building trust and revealing aspects of oneself at a pace that feels right for the relationship is essential for creating an authentic and secure connection.

ooo

Lara and Chris had been messaging on a dating app for a few weeks. Their conversations had started with shared interests in music and movies, but Lara decided to deepen the connection by sharing more personal aspects of her life. In a message, she opened up about her recent journey of self-discovery after a career change, which was both challenging and rewarding.

Reading Lara's story, Chris felt a more profound sense of connection. He appreciated her openness and, feeling a sense of trust, shared his own experience of moving to a new city and how it pushed him out of his comfort zone. This exchange marked a shift from casual chatting to a more meaningful dialogue.

Both Lara and Chris were cautious yet authentic in their sharing. They respected each other's pace in revealing personal stories, gradually building trust. Their conversation demonstrated a balance of vulnerability and discretion, allowing for a genuine connection that felt safe. By opening up at a comfortable pace, they were able to create a more profound and secure bond, typical of relationships rooted in authenticity and mutual understanding.

ooo

Keeping the Momentum

Finally, the art of crafting engaging conversations online involves knowing how to maintain momentum. This means knowing when to introduce new topics when to delve deeper into a discussion, and when to inject humor or change the tone. It's a delicate balance, akin to the ebb and flow of a dance, where both partners move in harmony, responsive to each other's cues.

In this part of the digital courtship journey, the goal is not just to communicate but to connect, to transform digital words into a pathway towards a real, tangible relationship.

ooo

After several weeks of messaging, Sophia and Ethan found their online conversations to be a highlight of their days. Ethan had a knack for keeping the conversation lively. He paid attention to the flow of their chats, introducing new topics when discussions started to wane. One evening, when the conversation about favorite movies started to peter out, he smoothly transitioned to talking about cooking, another shared interest, by sending a photo of his latest culinary experiment.

Sophia appreciated Ethan's ability to inject humor at just the right moments, often brightening her day with a witty remark or a funny anecdote. She reciprocated by sharing funny stories from her day, keeping the mood light and enjoyable.

They also knew when to delve deeper. One night, when Sophia expressed concerns about her job, Ethan responded with empathy, sharing his own experiences and offering support. This deepened their bond, showing that they could rely on each other for more than casual banter.

Their digital conversations were a dance of topics and emotions. Each knew when to step forward and when to follow, continually responsive to each other's cues. This ability to maintain momentum in their conversations turned their online interaction into a meaningful connection, laying the groundwork for a relationship that went beyond the digital realm.

ooo

Part 2

When to Transition from Online to In-Person

"The beauty of genuine conversation lies in the unknown
where discovery and learning are right around the
corner."

– Bryant H. McGill

Next, we explore the significant decision of transitioning
from an online connection to an in-person meeting. This
moment is a crucial turning point in the narrative of
modern dating, a juncture where the potential of the
virtual world meets the reality of the physical one.

Assessing the Right Moment

Deciding when to transition from online messaging to a
real-world encounter is nuanced and layered. It's akin to a
strategic game in which each move is deliberate and
adaptable to the evolving situation. The timing of this
transition isn't about a predefined period but the quality
and depth of the connection established. It involves
interpreting cues, understanding both parties' comfort
levels and gauging the conversation's natural progression.

ooo

Mia and Jordan had been messaging on a dating app for a
couple of weeks. Their conversations had evolved from
playful banter to more substantial exchanges about their
lives and interests. Jordan sensed a genuine connection but
was mindful of the timing for suggesting a face-to-face
meeting. He listened to Mia's responses, looking for

indications of her comfort level with the idea of meeting in person.

One evening, as they discussed their favorite local coffee shops, Mia casually mentioned that she hadn't tried a particular café Jordan loved. Seizing the opportunity, Jordan suggested, "Maybe we could check it out together this weekend?" His invitation was casual yet clear, offering a specific plan but leaving room for her to decide.

Mia, who had enjoyed their conversations and felt ready for the next step, enthusiastically agreed. Jordan's approach was thoughtful and respectful, showing that he was attuned to the natural progression of their connection. His careful consideration in assessing the right moment laid a solid foundation for their first real-world encounter, reflecting a mutual readiness to take their burgeoning relationship beyond the digital realm.

ooo

Building a Foundation of Trust

Establishing a foundation of trust and mutual interest is essential before suggesting an in-person meeting. This phase involves understanding the subtle dynamics of online communication. Are the exchanges becoming increasingly personal and open? Is there a sense of excitement and anticipation about the prospect of meeting? These are signs that both parties are ready to take the next step.

ooo

Rebecca and Tom had been messaging each other on a dating app for several weeks. Their initial casual conversations had gradually evolved into deeper, more personal exchanges. Rebecca found herself sharing details about her aspirations and daily life, and Tom reciprocated with stories from his own experiences. They discovered shared values and interests, and their messages became highlights of their days.

Rebecca noticed that their communication had grown increasingly open and genuine. They expressed excitement about their similar interests and often hinted at exploring these activities together. When Tom shared his experiences volunteering at a local animal shelter, a cause close to Rebecca's heart, she felt a surge of connection and trust.

One evening, when discussing a new exhibit at an art gallery they both wanted to visit, Tom suggested, "Perhaps we could see it together this weekend?" Rebecca, feeling a strong foundation of trust and mutual interest, agreed with a sense of anticipation. Their careful, respectful communication laid the groundwork for this next step, suggesting a real-world meeting feel like a natural and exciting progression of their growing bond.

ooo

Navigating the Hurdle of Expectations

Transitioning from online to in-person can come with a host of expectations, both expressed and unspoken. It's crucial to manage these expectations realistically. It's important to recognize that the person you've connected with online may not exactly match their digital persona in real life and be open to the delight of discovering their true self.

ooo

Grace and Leo had been communicating online for a month, their rapport growing steadily through shared jokes and stories. As they planned their first in-person meeting, both felt excitement and nervousness. Grace, in particular, pondered how Leo would compare to his online persona, which she had grown fond of.

On the day of their meeting, Grace reminded herself to manage her expectations. She knew that the nuances of in-person interactions could differ from digital exchanges. As they met at a local café, there was an initial awkwardness, a stark contrast to their effortless online conversations.

However, as they settled into the meeting, Grace discovered new aspects of Leo—his warm laughter, thoughtful mannerisms, and the way his eyes lit up when discussing his passions. While he was not exactly as she had imagined from their online interactions, these new dimensions added depth to his personality.

By keeping an open mind and managing her expectations, Grace allowed herself to appreciate Leo's true self beyond the digital portrayal. This approach turned their first meeting into an enjoyable experience, filled with genuine discovery and connection rather than disappointment over unmet expectations.

ooo

The Proposal: Timing and Approach

The art of proposing an in-person meeting is about timing and approach. The proposal should feel like a natural next step rather than a sudden leap. It could be tied to a shared interest discussed online or a casual suggestion to continue an engaging conversation over coffee.

ooo

Ellie and Nathan had been connecting through an online dating platform because of their mutual love for jazz music and old movies. Their conversations were always lively, filled with recommendations and anecdotes. After a particularly engaging chat about a jazz band that both had recently discovered, Nathan sensed it was the right moment to propose a meeting in person.

Casually, at the end of their conversation, he wrote, "I heard that jazz band we like is playing downtown this Friday. I was thinking of going. Would you be interested in joining me?" His approach was non-intrusive yet direct, linking the suggestion to a topic they were both passionate about.

Ellie, who had also been feeling the natural progression of their connection, was delighted by the suggestion. The proposal didn't feel out of the blue; it was a natural extension of what they had already shared. Nathan's timing and approach made the invitation feel comfortable and exciting rather than pressured. This careful consideration in proposing a real-world encounter echoed the thoughtful and genuine connection they had already established online.

ooo

Preparing for the In-Person Dynamic

Preparing for the shift in dynamics from online to in-person is key. In the digital world, we have the luxury of time to craft our responses and the shield of a screen to hide our immediate reactions. An in-person meeting removes these layers, revealing the unfiltered version of ourselves. This transition involves embracing the authenticity and spontaneity of real-life interactions and preparing oneself for a different, more direct mode of communication.

ooo

Before their first in-person meeting, Sarah reflected on the differences between their online interactions and what was to come. In their digital exchanges, she appreciated the time to think through her responses, often rewording texts to capture her thoughts perfectly. The upcoming face-to-face meeting, however, wouldn't offer this buffer. She knew that in-person conversations flow in real-time, with all the natural pauses, expressions, and spontaneous reactions.

To prepare, Sarah reminded herself to embrace the authenticity of the moment. She practised mindfulness, calming her nerves, and setting an intention to be present and genuine during the meeting. Sarah also prepared some conversation starters based on their previous chats to ease any initial awkwardness.

As she met Alex at the coffee shop, she took a deep breath and allowed the conversation to unfold naturally. The first few minutes were a bit stilted, but their dialogue soon flowed more freely. Sarah found that, without the screen as a barrier, she enjoyed the immediacy of their interaction – the shared laughter, the unspoken understanding conveyed through a glance, and the unfiltered glimpses into each other's personalities. Embracing this new dynamic, Sarah and Alex discovered a different, more vibrant dimension to their connection, one that could only be experienced in the spontaneity of real-life interactions.

ooo

Do's and Don'ts

Do's:

1. **Be Genuine in Your Opening Message.** Show that you've engaged with their profile and are interested in them as people.

2. **Maintain a Balanced Conversation:** Share your stories and interests and be curious about theirs.

3. **Show Vulnerability:** Share personal stories and genuine interests to deepen the connection.

4. **Keep the Conversation Lively:** Introduce new topics and inject humor to maintain momentum.

5. **Assess the Right Moment for Meeting:** Look for cues and mutual comfort levels before suggesting an in-person meeting.

Don'ts:

1. **Don't Use Generic Opening Lines:** Avoid messages that feel impersonal and unengaging.

2. **Don't Dominate the Conversation:** Ensure there's a balance of give and take in the dialogue.

3. **Don't Overshare Too Soon:** Be mindful of the pace at which you're revealing personal information.

4. **Don't Let the Conversation Stagnate:** Avoid sticking to the same topics and be willing to explore new discussion areas.

5. **Don't Rush the Transition to In-Person:** Ensure both parties are comfortable, and the timing feels natural.

Chapter 3

The First Date
- Setting the Stage for Success

Part 1

Pre-Date Preparations: Mindset and Expectations

"Expectation is the root of all heartache."

– William Shakespeare

In this part of the journey, we navigate the pivotal chapter of the first date, a moment rich with possibility and nuanced challenges. Preparing for it goes beyond choosing attire or venue; it delves into the realms of mindset and expectations, setting the stage for a meaningful encounter.

Cultivating the Right Mindset

The first date begins long before the actual meeting – it starts in the mind. It's about cultivating an open, curious, and grounded mindset. Embracing the notion of exploration over evaluation can alleviate anxiety and create a more relaxed, authentic interaction. Viewing the date as an opportunity to learn about someone new rather than as a high-pressure assessment can transform the experience.

ooo

As Sarah prepared for her first date with Ben, she felt a mix of excitement and nervousness. Their online conversations were engaging, and she genuinely looked forward to meeting him in person. Yet, the thought of a first date brought a familiar flutter of anxiety.

To ease her nerves, Sarah decided to adopt a different mindset. Instead of viewing the date as a make-or-break compatibility assessment, she saw it as an opportunity for exploration. She reminded herself that, like an intriguing chapter in a book, this date was a chance to learn more about Ben, his experiences, and his perspective on life.

Sarah's mindset shift became evident as they sat across from each other in a cosy café. She asked open-ended questions, eager to uncover the layers of Ben's personality. She listened attentively, not just to his words but to the nuances of his expressions and gestures.

This change in mindset had a remarkable effect. Sarah and Ben felt more relaxed and authentic. The date flowed naturally, with moments of laughter, shared stories, and genuine connection. By the end of the evening, Sarah realised that she had not only enjoyed the date but had also gained valuable insights into the person sitting across from her.

Cultivating the mindset of exploration transformed the first date from a high-pressure evaluation into a relaxed and enjoyable interaction, setting the stage for the possibility of something meaningful developing.

ooo

Managing Expectations

Expectations profoundly impact our experiences. It is crucial to manage expectations realistically on a first date. Acknowledge the excitement and hope, but temper them with the understanding that not every date will lead to a profound connection. This balance helps prevent the weight of unrealistic expectations from overshadowing the experience.

ooo

As Emily got ready for her first date with James, she couldn't help but feel a sense of anticipation. Their online conversations had been delightful, and she found herself looking forward to the evening with a mixture of excitement and hope. She had imagined various scenarios of how the date might unfold, and each one seemed filled with potential.

James was already waiting at their table when she arrived at the cosy restaurant. They exchanged warm smiles and greetings, and for a moment, Emily's heart skipped a beat. She was drawn to his charisma and charm.

However, as the evening progressed, Emily began to notice that the connection she had imagined during their online interactions wasn't as immediate as she had hoped. James was a great conversationalist, but subtle differences in their values and interests became more apparent in person.

In the past, Emily might have felt disappointed and disheartened by this realisation. However, she had learned the importance of managing her expectations realistically. She understood that not every date would lead to an instant and profound connection.

Instead of dwelling on the gap between her expectations and reality, Emily focused on enjoying the moment. She appreciated James for his company and the enjoyable conversation they shared. By the end of the evening, they both agreed that while they might not be the perfect match romantically, they had still had a pleasant time.

Emily left the date with a sense of contentment, knowing that managing her expectations had allowed her to fully appreciate the experience for what it was—an opportunity to meet someone new and enjoy an evening of engaging conversation.

ooo

The Power of First Impressions

First impressions on a date are crucial. They begin with how you present yourself, not just in terms of attire but also demeanour, body language, and the energy you bring. A positive attitude, a genuine smile, and open body language can set a welcoming tone for the encounter.

ooo

As the door to the coffee shop swung open, Mark scanned the room for a glimpse of his date, Sarah. He had arrived a few minutes early and decided to wait near the entrance. It had been a while since he'd been on a blind date, and he couldn't help feeling a mix of excitement and nervousness.

Moments later, Sarah walked in. Her eyes met Mark's, and she offered a warm smile. Mark was immediately struck by the positive energy radiating from her. As she approached, he couldn't help but notice how her smile seemed genuine, reaching her eyes.

Their greeting was effortless, and both shared light laughter while exchanging pleasantries. Mark appreciated Sarah's open and inviting body language, signalling her comfort and interest in the encounter.

As they settled into a cosy corner of the coffee shop, Mark couldn't help but reflect on the power of first impressions. Sarah's friendly demeanour, authentic smile, and open body language had set a welcoming tone for their date. It had put him at ease, allowing for a more relaxed and enjoyable conversation.

Throughout their date, Mark and Sarah continued to connect, sharing stories and laughter. While they both knew that first impressions were just the beginning of their journey, they also understood that a positive start laid a strong foundation for future interactions.

Mark left their first meeting optimistic and grateful that a positive attitude, a genuine smile, and open body language can work wonders in creating a favourable first impression.

ooo

The Role of Research

A bit of pre-date research can be beneficial. This doesn't mean an exhaustive investigation but reviewing previous conversations and shared interests to aid in crafting thoughtful and engaging dialogue. This preparation shows genuine interest and can lead to more meaningful and personalised conversations.

ooo

As the day of their first date approached, Emily decided to do some pre-date research. She had met Alex on a dating app, and their conversations flowed smoothly. They discovered shared interests in hiking and a love for indie music. Emily wanted their first meeting to be special and engaging, so she decided to review their previous chats.

Emily scrolled through their messages, noting the topics they had discussed. She remembered Alex mentioning his recent hiking adventure in a nearby national park and his passion for discovering new indie bands. Armed with this information, Emily formulated a plan.

On the day of their date, as they sat across from each other in a cosy cafe, Emily decided to kick-start the conversation. She asked Alex about his hiking adventures, expressing genuine interest in the details of his favorite trails and memorable moments. A smile spread across Alex's face as he shared his experiences, feeling appreciated and heard.

Later in the conversation, Emily mentioned a local indie music festival that weekend, subtly incorporating their shared interest. Alex's eyes lit up as they discussed their favorite indie bands and the possibility of attending the festival together.

Their date was a success, with Emily and Alex feeling a deep connection and genuine interest in each other's lives. Emily's pre-date research allowed her to craft thoughtful and engaging dialogue, creating a more meaningful and personalised experience for both. It was a reminder that a bit of preparation can go a long way in building a connection.

ooo

Setting Personal Boundaries

Understanding and respecting personal boundaries, yours and your date's, is key. It involves being clear about what you are comfortable with and communicating your boundaries if necessary. Respecting your date's limits creates a safe and comfortable environment for both parties.

ooo

Sarah and Mark sat at a charming corner table in a dimly lit restaurant, and their first date was off to a promising start. They shared stories, laughter, and a delicious meal. The conversation flowed effortlessly, creating a connection between them.

As the evening progressed, Sarah noticed that the conversation began to take a more intimate turn. Mark started asking questions that delved into personal and sensitive topics. While Sarah appreciated his curiosity, she also felt a need to set some personal boundaries.

Sarah addressed the situation with a warm smile. "Mark, I'm really enjoying our conversation, but there are some topics I prefer to keep private, especially on a first date. I hope you understand."

Mark, who had been genuinely interested in getting to know Sarah better, immediately understood and respected her boundaries. He apologised if he had made her uncomfortable and shifted the conversation to lighter, more comfortable subjects.

Sarah's assertiveness in setting her personal boundaries not only ensured her comfort but also strengthened their connection. Mark admired her honesty and felt more at ease knowing that Sarah was open about her preferences. This subtle yet important moment contributed to a successful and respectful first date.

ooo

The Art of Conversation

The first-date conversation is an art. It involves balancing talking and listening, sharing stories and asking questions, revealing oneself while also discovering the other. This balance is essential for creating a connection that goes beyond superficial small talk.

ooo

John and Emily found themselves in a cosy coffee shop on a crisp autumn afternoon. It was their first date, and as they sipped their lattes, they embarked on a journey of conversation.

Emily, intrigued by John's profile, where he mentioned his love for hiking, decided to steer the conversation in that direction. She asked, "John, you mentioned you're passionate about hiking. Do you have a favorite trail or a memorable hiking experience you'd like to share?"

John's eyes lit up as he began recounting a challenging hike he had undertaken in the Rockies. He vividly described the breathtaking views, the sense of accomplishment, and the camaraderie among fellow hikers. In turn, Emily shared her hiking stories, and soon they discussed their favorite outdoor destinations.

Their conversation flowed effortlessly from hiking to travel, hobbies to life goals. They found a natural rhythm, taking turns to speak and listen attentively. It wasn't just about impressing each other with their stories but about genuinely connecting through shared interests and experiences.

As the sun dipped below the horizon, they realised that hours had flown by. What began as a coffee date had transformed into a captivating conversation that left them both eager to explore more chapters of their connection. The art of conversation had woven a tapestry of shared experiences and mutual understanding, setting the stage for a promising journey ahead.

ooo

Embracing Uncertainty

Finally, it's important to embrace the uncertainty that comes with a first date. Acknowledging that not every date will go as planned and being open to the unexpected can transform anxiety into excitement. It's about enjoying the journey, regardless of the destination.

ooo

Sarah and Mark had been chatting online for a few weeks and decided it was time to meet in person. They had chosen a quaint restaurant for their first date. As Sarah nervously waited at their agreed-upon meeting spot, she couldn't help but feel a sense of uncertainty.

Mark arrived, and they greeted each other with smiles. They began their first-date conversation as they settled into their seats at the restaurant. The initial awkwardness gradually gave way to comfortable exchanges. However, just as they were getting into a deep discussion about their favorite books, the restaurant's power unexpectedly went out, plunging the place into darkness.

Both Sarah and Mark laughed at the unforeseen turn of events. Without missing a beat, Mark pulled out his phone, turned on the flashlight, and they continued their conversation by the soft glow of the screen. It turned out to be a memorable and unique experience, and they learned a lot about each other during those candlelit moments.

The power eventually came back on, but the laughter and connection they had shared during the blackout remained. Sarah and Mark realised that embracing the uncertainty of a first date could lead to unexpected and delightful moments, making the journey of getting to know each other all the more exciting.

Part 2

Navigating the First Encounter: Do's and Don'ts

"The first duty of love is to listen."

– Paul Tillich

As we progress to the actual first date, this part focuses on the nuanced choreography of the encounter itself. We delve into the do's and don'ts that can significantly influence this initial meeting.

The Do's: Creating a Positive Experience

Punctuality and Respect for Time: Being on time for your date shows respect and sets a positive tone for the evening. Small factors like punctuality can significantly impact the overall experience.

Engaging and Attentive Listening: Transform ordinary conversations into meaningful exchanges by showing genuine interest in what your date is saying. Deeply engaging with your date's perspectives can significantly enhance the connection.

Maintaining a Balanced Conversation: Dialogue should flow freely and harmoniously. While sharing about yourself is important, also encourage your date to share their stories and views.

Appropriate Body Language: Non-verbal cues are as important as words. Open body language, maintaining eye contact, and nodding in understanding can foster a sense of connection and attentiveness.

Being Yourself: Authenticity is key. Be genuine instead of trying to impress with an exaggerated version of yourself. Authentic interactions often lead to more meaningful connections.

ooo

For their first date, John and Emily decided to meet at a cosy cafe. John arrived a few minutes early and chose a table with a view of the picturesque park across the street, where he knew Emily enjoyed spending time.

When Emily arrived, she noticed John was already there, waiting with a warm smile. They greeted each other, and John pulled out the chair for Emily, a small gesture that made her feel appreciated.

Throughout the date, they engaged in a conversation that felt like a natural flow of thoughts and ideas. Emily shared stories about her recent hiking adventure, and John listened attentively, asking questions and showing genuine interest in her experiences. Emily, in turn, asked John about his passion for painting, and he enthusiastically described his latest art project.

Their body language also spoke volumes. They maintained eye contact, and their open postures conveyed a sense of comfort and connection. They both felt at ease being themselves, and the authenticity of their interaction deepened their connection.

As the evening came to a close, they agreed that the date had been a great success. John expressed his interest in seeing Emily again, and she smiled warmly, indicating her agreement. They left the cafe, looking forward to their next meeting, with the feeling that this first date had set a positive and promising tone for their budding relationship.

ooo

Avoiding Common Pitfalls

Overemphasis on Physical Appearance or Material Success: While first impressions matter, focusing solely on physical or material aspects can be superficial. Look beyond surface-level attributes to deeper qualities.

Dominating the Conversation: Avoid monopolising the conversation. Striking a balance between speaking and listening ensures a two-way exchange and mutual engagement.

Bringing Up Controversial Topics Prematurely: While discussing values and beliefs is important, the first date might not be the best time for potentially polarising topics. Approach such topics with care and tact.

Checking Your Phone Constantly: In today's digital age, constant phone checking can signal disinterest and disrespect. Stay present and engaged with your date.

Setting Unrealistic Expectations: Avoid projecting too far into the future or idealising your date based on limited information. Manage expectations realistically to avoid potential disappointments.

ooo

Lisa and Michael had arranged to meet for dinner at a trendy restaurant. As soon as they sat down, Michael couldn't help but comment on Lisa's appearance, saying, "You look absolutely stunning tonight."

While the compliment was well-intentioned, Michael continued to focus on Lisa's physical attributes throughout the evening, occasionally steering the conversation back to her appearance. Lisa felt uncomfortable with the constant emphasis on her looks and wished they could discuss more substantial topics.

Michael also dominated the conversation with stories about his achievements and career, leaving little room for Lisa to share her experiences and perspectives. He also brought up controversial political topics without much preamble, leading to a tense discussion that left them uneasy.

Throughout the date, Michael frequently checked his phone for messages and notifications, making Lisa feel he wasn't fully present. The constant distraction hindered their ability to connect on a deeper level.

As the evening concluded, Lisa appreciated the compliments but couldn't shake the feeling that Michael was focused on superficial things. She decided to be honest with him about her concerns, expressing her desire for a more balanced and meaningful conversation. While Michael seemed surprised, he appreciated Lisa's feedback and agreed to approach their next date differently.

ooo

The Follow-Up: The Art of Closure

The conclusion of a first date can set the tone for future interactions. Whether there's a connection or not, honesty and respect are paramount. If you feel a connection, express interest in meeting again, or communicate your feelings politely and honestly if not. This approach ensures clarity and respect, regardless of the outcome.

ooo

Sarah and David's first date had gone well. They had a delightful conversation, shared laughter, and discovered several common interests. As they walked to their respective cars, they stopped by the park entrance where they had initially met.

David turned to Sarah and said, "I had a fantastic time tonight, Sarah. I'd love to see you again. Would you be interested in going out for dinner next weekend?"

Sarah appreciated David's straightforward approach and felt a connection. She smiled and replied, "I had a great time, too, David. I'd love to go to dinner with you next weekend. Let's plan it!"

They exchanged contact information and parted ways, excited about their future date. Their clear and respectful communication had set a positive tone for what they hoped would be a promising relationship.

ooo

Do's and Don'ts

Do's:

1. **Cultivate an Open Mindset:** Approach the date with curiosity and openness, viewing it as an opportunity to learn about someone new.

2. **Manage Expectations:** Keep a realistic perspective, understanding that not every date will lead to a profound connection.

3. **Make a Positive First Impression:** Present yourself well in terms of attire, demeanour, and body language to set a welcoming tone.

4. **Do Pre-Date Research:** Review previous conversations and shared interests to prepare for engaging in personalised dialogue.

5. **Set Personal Boundaries:** Be clear about your comfort levels and communicate your boundaries respectfully if needed.

6. **Master the Art of Conversation:** Balance talking and listening, and share stories and questions to discover each other genuinely.

7. **Embrace Uncertainty:** Be open to the unexpected and enjoy the journey of the first date, regardless of the outcome.

8. **Express Interest for Future Interaction:** If you feel a connection, clearly express your interest in meeting again.

Don'ts:

1. **Avoid Overemphasis on Superficial Aspects:** Don't focus solely on physical appearance or material success; seek deeper qualities.

2. **Don't Dominate the Conversation:** Ensure a two-way exchange and mutual engagement in the conversation.

3. **Refrain from Controversial Topics Prematurely:** Approach sensitive topics with care and tact, especially on a first date.

4. **Avoid Constant Phone Checking:** Stay present and engaged with your date, avoiding distractions from your phone.

5. **Don't Set Unrealistic Expectations:** Avoid idealizing your date based on limited information and manage your expectations.

6. **Avoid Superficial Focus:** Aim for more substantial conversations instead of focusing only on appearance or achievements.

7. **Don't Rush the Closure.** At the end of the date, Be respectful and honest in your communication, whether you feel a connection or not.

Chapter 4

Reading Between the Lines – Understanding Non-Verbal Cues

Part 1

The Language of Body Language

"The most important thing in communication is hearing what isn't said."

– Peter Drucker

Let's explore the realm of non-verbal communication and delve into the nuanced and often subconscious world of body language during dating encounters. This section aims to decode the silent yet expressive language of the body, providing key insights into understanding and interpreting these subtle cues.

The Unspoken Dialogue

Body language is vital to human communication, often conveying more than words. On a date, these non-verbal cues can offer invaluable insights into a person's feelings and intentions. Recognising the importance of these subtle signals is crucial in understanding your date's reactions and emotions.

The Basics of Body Language

Facial Expressions: The face is a canvas for emotions. Smiles, frowns, raised eyebrows, and eye contact (or lack thereof) can reveal a person's interest, discomfort, amusement, or scepticism. Correctly interpreting these cues can help you better understand your date's reactions and feelings.

Posture: Posture communicates confidence, openness, and interest. Leaning in slightly may indicate interest and attentiveness, while crossed arms or a slouched posture might suggest disinterest or discomfort.

Gestures: Hand movements, nods, and shifts in seating can accentuate or contradict spoken words. Open hand gestures suggest honesty and engagement, while fidgeting or avoiding eye contact could indicate discomfort or disinterest.

Context and Congruence

Context is key to understanding body language. A gesture or expression must be interpreted within the overall situation and verbal communication. For example, crossed arms might indicate defensiveness in one context but could be a comfortable posture in another.

Congruence between verbal and non-verbal communication is also critical. Aligned words and body language reinforce the message, while discrepancies can be revealing, such as when verbal expressions of interest are contradicted by body language.

Cultural Variations

It is essential to recognize that interpretations of body language can vary across cultures. What signifies agreement or politeness in one culture might mean something entirely different in another. Awareness of and sensitivity to these cultural differences is crucial in the increasingly globalised dating world.

The Art of Observing

Developing the skill to read body language involves becoming a keen observer. It is vital to pay attention to subtleties, fleeting expressions, and the overall demeanour of your date. This observation is about gathering information to understand the person better rather than making snap judgments.

Enhancing Your Own Body Language

Finally, being aware of your own body language is as important as reading others'. Reflecting on how you express yourself non-verbally and perhaps adjusting your cues to ensure they align with your intentions can significantly improve the quality of your interactions. This self-awareness enhances not only your dating experiences but your interpersonal skills in general.

ooo

Samantha and Daniel were on their first date at a cosy restaurant. Throughout the evening, their body language spoke volumes, revealing much about their feelings and connection.

As they sat across from each other, their facial expressions were telling. Samantha's eyes sparkled with genuine interest as Daniel shared a childhood story, and her warm smile indicated her amusement. Daniel, in turn, frequently made eye contact with Samantha, raising his expressive eyebrows in enthusiasm as she recounted a recent travel adventure.

Their posture was another indicator of their connection. Samantha leaned in slightly when Daniel spoke, a subtle sign of attentiveness and engagement. Daniel, mirroring her posture, displayed a similar interest. Their open postures created an inviting and comfortable atmosphere.

Gestures also played a role in their unspoken dialogue. Samantha occasionally reached out to lightly touch Daniel's arm while sharing a particularly personal story, emphasising her trust and connection with him. Daniel responded with gentle nods and mirrored her gestures, reinforcing their rapport.

What was particularly noteworthy was the congruence between their verbal and non-verbal communication. When Samantha expressed excitement about a shared interest, her facial expressions and gestures echoed her words, creating a harmonious message. Similarly, Daniel's body language aligned perfectly with his verbal expressions of admiration for Samantha's adventurous spirit.

Samantha and Daniel's ability to read each other's body language allowed them to connect on a deeper level, reinforcing the positive atmosphere of their date. Their silent yet expressive conversation clearly played a crucial role in building a promising connection.

ooo

Part 2

Detecting Interest and Disinterest

"Eyes speak louder than words."

– Unknown

A key question is how to discern signs of interest and disinterest through nonverbal cues. This exploration focuses on uncovering the deeper meanings beneath surface-level observations.

Deciphering Signs of Interest

Positive Facial Expressions: A genuine smile often reaches the eyes, creating 'crow's feet' – a reliable sign of genuine pleasure. Frequent eye contact and nodding suggest engagement and interest in the conversation.

Mirroring Body Language: Subconsciously mimicking your posture or gestures is a classic sign of rapport, indicating empathy and connection.

Proximity and Touch: Leaning in during conversation and occasional, appropriate touches (like a light tap on the arm) can signal comfort and interest. It's crucial to ensure that such gestures are welcome and reciprocated.

Open Body Posture: An open posture, with uncrossed arms and legs and a forward-leaning position, suggests openness and interest, reflecting a comfort level and willingness to engage more deeply.

Increased Attention and Focus: Paying undivided attention and not getting distracted by surroundings or phones shows genuine interest in the interaction.

Recognising Signs of Disinterest

Closed Body Language: Crossed arms, averted eyes, and a generally closed-off posture can indicate disinterest or discomfort.

Lack of Facial Engagement: Limited facial expressions or forced smiles can signal a lack of genuine interest or enjoyment in the interaction.

Frequent Distractions: Constantly checking their phone, looking around the room, or seeming disengaged are clear signs of a lack of interest.

Minimal Physical Engagement: A lack of physical closeness, such as leaning back or maintaining a noticeable distance, can be a non-verbal cue of disinterest. This distancing might be a subconscious attempt to create a barrier.

Short, Non-Expansive Responses: Short answers without elaboration or enthusiasm in a conversation can indicate a lack of interest, signifying minimal investment in the interaction.

Navigating Mixed Signals

In the complex dating world, signals can sometimes be mixed or hard to interpret. Looking at the broader context and patterns over time, rather than relying on a single interaction, can provide a clearer picture of a person's feelings and intentions.

Responding to Disinterest

If signs point to disinterest, it's important to approach the situation with respect and understanding. It might mean gracefully ending the date or conversation or simply changing the approach to see if the dynamic improves.

ooo

Alex and Taylor's first date was a whirlwind of emotions, and they both had mixed feelings about their connection.

During their dinner, they exchanged stories and jokes. Taylor frequently made eye contact with Alex, nodding enthusiastically as they spoke about shared interests. This suggested genuine engagement and interest. In response, Alex mirrored Taylor's body language and even playfully touched their arm while sharing a funny anecdote, creating a sense of rapport.

However, there were moments of uncertainty. Taylor occasionally glanced at their phone and seemed distracted, which contrasted with their otherwise enthusiastic demeanour. Alex noticed this and couldn't help but feel a pang of doubt. Was Taylor truly interested, or were they just being polite?

As the evening continued, Taylor's responses became shorter and less detailed. They started leaning back, creating more physical distance between them and Alex. This change in body language raised questions for Alex. Was Taylor growing disinterested, or was there another explanation?

The mixed signals left Alex and Taylor in a state of uncertainty. While some interest was clear, intermittent signs of disinterest cast a shadow of doubt.

In situations like this, where signals are mixed, it's essential to consider the broader context. A single date might not provide a complete picture of a person's feelings. Perhaps Taylor had a hectic day and was momentarily distracted. Or maybe there were other factors at play. Alex decided to give it some time and plan a second date to see if the dynamic would clarify.

Understanding non-verbal cues is crucial, but it's equally important to navigate mixed signals with patience and open communication to determine the true nature of the connection.

Do's and Don'ts

Do's:

1. **Observe Facial Expressions:** Pay attention to genuine smiles, raised eyebrows, and eye contact to gauge interest and emotions.

2. **Notice Posture:** Look for open postures, like leaning in, which may indicate interest and attentiveness.

3. **Interpret Gestures:** Be aware of hand movements, nods, and seating shifts that can complement or contradict spoken words.

4. **Consider Context and Congruence:** Interpret body language within the overall situation and ensure it aligns with verbal communication.

5. **Be Culturally Sensitive:** Recognize that body language can vary across cultures and adapt your interpretations accordingly.

6. **Develop Observation Skills:** To enhance your ability to read body language, be a keen observer of subtleties and expressions.

7. **Be Aware of Your Own Body Language:** Reflect on how you express yourself non-verbally and adjust to ensure alignment with your intentions.

8. **Respond Appropriately to Interest Signs:** If you detect positive cues like mirroring, proximity, and open posture, reciprocate to build rapport.

9. **Navigate Mixed Signals with Patience:** To better understand intentions, consider the broader context and patterns over time.

Don'ts:

1. **Don't Misinterpret Closed Body Language:** Avoid jumping to conclusions about crossed arms or averted eyes without considering the context.

2. **Avoid Ignoring Facial Engagement:** Be cautious if your date shows limited facial expressions or forced smiles, as it might indicate disinterest.

3. **Don't Overlook Frequent Distractions:** Be aware if your date constantly checks their phone or seems disengaged.

4. **Avoid Disregarding Physical Distance:** Note if your date maintains a noticeable distance or leans back, as this could be a sign of disinterest.

5. **Don't Dismiss Short Responses:** Be mindful of brief answers without elaboration, which might signify a lack of investment in the interaction.

6. **Don't Force Interpretations:** Avoid making definitive judgments based on a single gesture or expression; look for consistent patterns.

7. **Don't Neglect Cultural Differences:** Be careful not to apply your cultural norms to someone from a different background.

8. **Don't Ignore Your Own Nonverbal Cues.** Be conscious of the signals your body language is sending.

9. **Don't React Hastily to Mixed Signals:** Avoid making quick decisions based on mixed or unclear signals; give the situation time to unfold.

Chapter 5

Communication is Key
- Building a Connection

Part 1

Effective Communication Strategies

"The way we communicate with others and with ourselves ultimately determines the quality of our lives."

– Anthony Robbins

Building and sustaining connections is an essential element of communication in dating. Effective communication is more than just exchanging words; it conveys feelings, shares experiences, and establishes a genuine connection.

The Foundation of Good Communication

Clarity of Expression: It is paramount to be transparent and articulate in expressing thoughts and feelings. This involves choosing words carefully, being honest, and avoiding ambiguity. Clarity is crucial in conveying complex ideas and emotions, making it vital to personal communication.

Active Listening: Active listening extends beyond merely hearing words; it involves understanding the underlying emotions and meanings. This means giving your full attention, showing genuine interest, and responding appropriately, demonstrating a deep engagement with your partner's perspectives.

Empathy and Understanding: Empathy is about putting oneself in the other person's shoes and understanding their feelings and perspectives, even if they differ from yours. Displaying empathy can significantly strengthen and authenticate a connection.

Enhancing Conversational Skills

Asking Open-Ended Questions: Open-ended questions encourage a free flow of ideas and show your interest in learning more about the person.

Storytelling and Sharing: Sharing experiences and stories makes conversations more engaging and relatable, helping to weave a more personal and meaningful connection.

Humor and Lightness: Humor can lighten the mood and enhance the enjoyment of the interaction. It is vital to ensure that the humor is appropriate and well-received by the other person.

Non-Verbal Communication

Body Language and Tone of Voice: Non-verbal elements like body language and tone of voice significantly impact how your messages are perceived. Positive non-verbal cues can make your conversation more engaging.

Eye Contact: Maintaining appropriate eye contact demonstrates confidence and interest and is a powerful tool for creating a connection.

Navigating Difficult Conversations

Handling Sensitive Topics: Approach sensitive topics with tact and sensitivity, creating a safe space for open sharing.

Conflict Resolution: Address conflicts calmly and constructively, focusing on understanding before being understood, to maintain and strengthen the connection.

Continuous Improvement

Feedback and Adaptation: Be open to feedback about your communication style. Self-awareness can significantly help you adapt and improve your interactions.

Practice and Reflection: Like any skill, effective communication improves with practice. Reflect on your conversations, learn from your experiences, and continually strive to enhance your communication abilities.

ooo

Sarah and Liam's first date had been going remarkably well. They found themselves engrossed in a conversation about their shared passion for hiking.

Eager to keep the conversation flowing, Liam asked an open-ended question. "Tell me about your most memorable hiking experience," he said, his eyes filled with genuine curiosity.

Sarah smiled, appreciating the opportunity to share a personal story. She recounted a thrilling hike through a lush forest, describing the sights, sounds, and the sense of accomplishment she felt at the summit. Her storytelling painted a vivid picture and allowed Liam to glimpse into her adventurous spirit.

Liam reciprocated by sharing his hiking adventure, with humorous mishaps that had them both laughing. Their conversation seamlessly transitioned from one story to another, creating an engaging exchange.

Throughout the evening, they interwove stories and personal anecdotes into their discussion. Their ability to share experiences and infuse humor into the conversation enhanced their connection. It wasn't just words they exchanged; it was a sense of shared experiences and a deeper understanding of each other.

Sarah and Liam's conversational skills, including asking open-ended questions, sharing stories, and adding humor, made their date memorable and enjoyable. These skills allowed them to form a genuine connection, laying a strong foundation for potential future encounters.

ooo

Part 2

Balancing Sharing and Listening

"Most people do not listen with the intent to understand; they listen with the intent to reply."

– Stephen R. Covey

Let's focus on the delicate equilibrium between sharing personal insights and listening actively. This balance is crucial for deepening understanding and fostering mutual respect in the context of dating and building connections.

Balanced Sharing

Self-Disclosure with Moderation: Sharing about oneself is essential for building intimacy but requires moderation. Gradually opening up and gauging the other person's reactions and comfort levels can create conversation intrigue and connection.

Reciprocity in Sharing: Conversations should be reciprocal. If you dominate the dialogue, pause and invite the other person to share. Encouraging your date to open up creates balance and mutual interest.

Vulnerability and Authenticity: Although being authentic and sharing one's true thoughts and feelings can be daunting, they are crucial for building trust and leading to a deeper, more meaningful connection.

Mastering the Skill of Listening

Active and Empathetic Listening: Truly listening is more than hearing words; it's understanding the emotions and intentions behind them. Show empathy and interest in what your date is sharing, reflect on what you've understood, and ask follow-up questions.

Reading Between the Lines: Pay attention to non-verbal cues and implied messages. Understanding what is left unsaid can be as important as what is spoken.

Resisting the Urge to Interrupt: Practice patience and allow your date to fully express themselves before responding, avoiding interrupting with your own story or opinion.

Navigating the Conversation Flow

Finding Common Ground: Seek topics of mutual interest. This means finding a common thread for enriching and engaging discussions, not necessarily avoiding disagreements.

The Dance of Conversation: A good conversation involves rhythm and coordination. Be attuned to the pace and direction of the dialogue, knowing when to delve deeper or lighten the mood.

Adjusting to Feedback: Be receptive to verbal and nonverbal feedback. If a topic seems uncomfortable, gracefully shift the conversation or explore further if a subject sparks interest.

The Role of Silence

Embracing Moments of Silence: Comfortable silences can be powerful, providing space to process and reflect. Not every moment needs to be filled with talk.

Using Silence to Reflect: Use brief pauses to gather your thoughts or consider your date's perspective, which will lead to more meaningful and considered responses.

Fostering Mutual Understanding

Balancing sharing and listening aims to create a dynamic of mutual understanding and respect. It's about creating a space where both individuals feel heard, valued, and connected. Effective communication in dating should honor both voices, creating a tapestry of shared experiences and mutual empathy.

ooo

Emily and Daniel sat across from each other in a cosy cafe, their conversation flowing effortlessly. As they sipped their coffee, Emily contemplated the delicate balance of sharing and listening.

Daniel, eager to get to know Emily better, began by sharing a personal story about his recent hiking adventure. He described the breathtaking mountain views and the serenity he felt at the summit. Emily listened intently, her eyes reflecting genuine interest.

After Daniel finished his story, he turned the conversation toward Emily. "I'd love to hear about your outdoor adventures," he said with a warm smile.

Emily appreciated Daniel's genuine curiosity and decided to share a hiking experience of her own. She recounted a memorable camping trip with friends, complete with humorous mishaps around the campfire. Daniel laughed along with her, clearly enjoying her storytelling.

As the conversation continued, they effortlessly alternated between sharing stories from their lives. They recognised the importance of self-disclosure with moderation, allowing each other to open up and deepen their connection gradually.

What struck Emily was Daniel's ability to create reciprocity in sharing. He didn't dominate the conversation with his own stories but actively invited her to share her experiences. This balanced approach made Emily feel valued and encouraged her to open up more.

Their date continued with a harmonious exchange of personal insights and shared laughter. The art of balanced sharing allowed Emily and Daniel to build a connection founded on mutual understanding and respect.

Do's and Don'ts

Do's:

1. **Express Clearly:** Be articulate and honest in expressing your thoughts and feelings to avoid ambiguity.

2. **Practice Active Listening:** Give full attention, show genuine interest, and respond appropriately to demonstrate engagement.

3. **Show Empathy:** Try to understand your date's feelings and perspectives, even if they differ from your own.

4. **Ask Open-Ended Questions:** Encourage a free flow of ideas and show interest in learning more about your date.

5. **Share Stories:** Make conversations engaging and relatable by sharing personal experiences.

6. **Use Humor Appropriately:** Lighten the mood with humor, ensuring it's appropriate and well-received.

7. **Be Aware of Nonverbal Cues.** Pay attention to body language and tone of voice, as they significantly impact communication.

8. **Maintain Eye Contact:** Demonstrate confidence and interest through appropriate eye contact.

9. **Handle Sensitive Topics Tactfully:** Approach delicate subjects with sensitivity and create a safe space for open sharing.

10. **Resolve Conflicts Constructively:** Address disagreements calmly and focus on understanding before being understood.

11. **Be Open to Feedback:** Adapt and improve your communication style based on feedback.

12.**Practice and Reflect:** Continuously work on enhancing your communication skills through practice and reflection.

Don'ts:

1. **Don't Be Vague or Misleading:** Avoid using unclear language that can lead to misunderstandings.

2. **Don't Just Hear, Listen:** Avoid passive listening; engage actively with what your date is saying.

3. **Don't Lack Empathy:** Avoid being indifferent to your date's feelings and perspectives.

4. **Don't Ask Only Closed Questions:** Avoid questions that lead to short, unelaborative answers.

5. **Don't Monopolize the Conversation:** Avoid talking about yourself excessively without giving your date a chance to share.

6. **Don't Misuse Humor:** Avoid inappropriate jokes or humor that might be offensive or misunderstood.

7. **Don't Ignore Body Language:** Avoid neglecting the non-verbal aspects of communication.

8. **Don't Avoid Eye Contact:** Avoid looking away frequently, which can signal disinterest or discomfort.

9. **Don't Insensitively Approach Delicate Topics:** Avoid being tactless when discussing sensitive subjects.

10.**Don't Escalate Conflicts:** Avoid reacting impulsively or aggressively during disagreements.

11.**Don't Dismiss Feedback:** Avoid being defensive or resistant to feedback about your communication style.

12.**Don't Stop Improving:** Avoid complacency; always look for ways to enhance how you

Chapter 6

The Follow-Up
- Post First Date Etiquette

Part 1

To Text or Not to Text: Post-Date Dilemma

"Patience is the calm acceptance that things can happen in a different order than the one you have in your mind."

– David G. Allen

The terrain of post-first-date communication is a period often marked by uncertainty and expectations. This part of the dating journey involves decoding social cues and making strategic decisions.

The Post-Date Communication Conundrum

After the first date, deciding whether to send a text and when can feel as complex as a strategic move in a high-stakes game. This dilemma reflects the uncertainties inherent in human interaction and requires a careful blend of empathy, timing, and social awareness. Understanding the subtle nuances of the date's conclusion and the signals sent during the encounter is key.

Timing and Tone

The decision of when to text depends on the tone and outcome of the first date. It's crucial to find the right timing that feels natural and considerate. The text's content should reflect the date's tone and capture the essence of your time together, showing engagement and presence.

The Initial Text: A Gesture of Appreciation

A simple, sincere message expressing gratitude for the date can be a safe yet thoughtful way to initiate post-date communication. The initial text sets the stage for further conversation, showing interest without applying pressure. The message should be clear, concise, and genuine, free from over-analysis or game-playing.

Reading the Response

The response to the initial text can provide significant insights. It's important to consider not just the content but also the timing and tone of the response. A prompt and enthusiastic reply might indicate mutual interest, while a delayed or lukewarm response could suggest hesitation. It's crucial to avoid jumping to conclusions and consider factors like the individual's communication style or daily schedule.

The Second Text: Gauging Interest

If the initial text is met with a positive response, sending a follow-up message can continue the conversation. This might involve referencing something discussed during the date or a light-hearted comment. The key is to keep the conversation flowing naturally. If the response is still positive and engaging, it could indicate mutual interest and the potential for a second date.

Navigating Silence

If the response is non-existent or lacklustre, it might be a sign to step back. Respect and understanding are essential. The lack of response does not necessarily reflect your worth or appeal but could be influenced by various factors in the other person's life.

The Delicate Dance of Post-Date Communication

Post-first-date texting is a delicate communication dance that requires a balance of interest, respect, and timing. It's about reading the situation, understanding the subtle cues, and responding considerately and authentically. This dance is intricate and nuanced, with each step carrying its weight and significance.

ooo

Sarah sat in her cosy living room, her thoughts consumed by her recent first date with Alex. It had been a fantastic evening filled with laughter, meaningful conversations, and an undeniable connection. But now, as she stared at her phone, she found herself amid the post-date communication conundrum.

She remembered how the date had ended—with a warm hug, a genuine smile, and Alex saying, "I had a wonderful time tonight." Sarah reciprocated the sentiment, and as she walked back to her car, her heart was aflutter with the possibility of something special.

Now, the question was whether to send a text. She knew the timing and tone were crucial. She wanted to convey her interest without appearing too eager. After thoughtful consideration, she decided on a simple message: "I had a great time, too. Thanks for a wonderful evening!"

Sarah hit send and waited anxiously. The minutes felt like hours as she wondered how Alex would respond. Would he share her enthusiasm? Was he feeling the same connection she did?

Finally, her phone lit up with a message notification. She opened it to find a reply from Alex: "I'm really glad to hear that, Sarah. I enjoyed our conversation a lot!"

Relief washed over Sarah. Alex's response was positive, and it seemed like he had enjoyed the date as much as she did. She decided to send a follow-up message, referencing a funny anecdote from their conversation. The conversation flowed naturally; before they knew it, they were chatting about their favorite travel destinations.

As the evening progressed, Sarah couldn't help but smile. The delicate dance of post-date communication had begun, and it felt like they were taking steps in harmony. While the future was uncertain, Sarah was excited about the possibilities, knowing that the key to this dance was mutual interest, respect, and genuine connection.

ooo

Part 2

Assessing Interest Levels: Signs and Signals

*"Interest speaks all sorts of tongues
and plays all kinds of characters."*
                                        – Latin Proverb

There is a subtle art of interpreting signs and signals after a first date to gauge mutual interest. This process involves keen observation and intuition to understand the underlying messages in social interactions.

Interpreting the Aftermath of the First Date

The period following the first date is often filled with questions and analyses about its success and the other person's interest. Deciphering post-date signals requires sifting through layers of information, much like unravelling a complex narrative to find the core truth.

The Importance of Communication Patterns

One of the first indicators of interest is the pattern of communication that follows the date. A continued and engaging conversation, with both parties initiating and responding eagerly, typically suggests mutual interest. Conversely, sporadic, short, or non-existent messages may indicate a lack of enthusiasm. Understanding these patterns requires considering the context, such as external factors affecting communication frequency.

Analysing In-Person and Digital Interactions

Responsiveness: The speed and enthusiasm of responses to texts or calls can be telling. Delayed or brief responses might signal disinterest, while prompt and detailed replies often indicate a desire to continue the connection.

Initiation: Consistent effort from both parties in initiating conversation suggests balanced interest. If only one person consistently initiates, it may indicate a disparity in interest levels.

Content of Communication: The substance of post-date conversations can reveal much about the connection. Superficial discussions versus deeper, more personal topics can indicate the level of comfort and interest in deepening the relationship.

Non-Verbal Cues and Subtle Indications

Non-verbal cues during subsequent dates can provide further insight into someone's interest. Observing body language, eye contact, and physical proximity can be as revealing as verbal communication. Subconscious indicators like maintaining eye contact or open body language can signal interest.

The Role of Patience and Perspective

Patience and perspective are important in assessing interest levels. Avoid jumping to conclusions based on limited data. Giving the relationship time to unfold naturally allows both parties to express their interest levels comfortably.

The Art of Moving Forward or Stepping Back

If signs indicate mutual interest, nurturing the budding relationship with care and open communication is the path forward. However, stepping back respectfully may be appropriate if indicators suggest a lack of interest. Maintaining dignity and respect for oneself and the other person is crucial in either scenario. Regardless of its outcome, every interaction offers valuable insights and learning opportunities.

ooo

Mark sat at his desk, his mind drifting back to his first date with Emily. They had met for coffee at a charming little cafe, and the conversation had flowed effortlessly. Mark couldn't help but feel a connection, and judging by Emily's laughter and the way she maintained eye contact, it seemed mutual.

The date ended with a warm hug and a promise to meet again. As Mark drove back home, he felt a mixture of excitement and anticipation. He was eager to see where this connection might lead.

In the days following their date, Mark carefully observed the signs and signals to assess Emily's interest. He remembered the patterns of communication—the way she texted him the very next day, expressing her enjoyment of their time together. They engaged in a lively conversation, sharing stories and interests.

The responsiveness in their messages had been encouraging, with both taking turns initiating conversations. Mark appreciated how Emily had shared more personal anecdotes, revealing her thoughts and aspirations.

Their second date had been equally enjoyable. They explored a nearby art gallery, discussing their favorite paintings and artists. Emily's body language had remained open, and she had often reached out to touch his arm as they talked.

Mark felt a growing sense of optimism as he reflected on these interactions. The signs and signals were aligning, indicating mutual interest. However, he also reminded himself of the importance of patience and perspective. It was still early, but he knew building a meaningful connection took time.

It was uncertain whether this budding relationship would flourish, but Mark was determined to embrace the journey. He understood that every interaction, every shared moment, was an opportunity to learn and grow, regardless of the outcome.

As he picked up his phone to send Emily a message, Mark couldn't help but smile. Assessing interest levels is an intricate dance, and he was ready to take the next step with confidence and enthusiasm.

Do's and Don'ts

Do's:

1. **Consider Timing for Post-Date Texts:** Choose a natural and considerate moment to text based on the date's outcome.

2. **Send a Sincere Initial Text:** Express gratitude for the date with a simple, sincere message.

3. **Read Responses Carefully:** To gauge interest, pay attention to the timing, tone, and content of the response.

4. **Continue the Conversation Naturally:** If the initial text is met positively, keep the conversation flowing with light-hearted or relevant topics.

5. **Respect Silence:** If there's no response or a lackluster reply, understand the signal and step back respectfully.

6. **Observe Communication Patterns:** Look for balanced effort in initiating and responding to conversations post-date.

7. **Analyze In-Person and Digital Interactions:** Consider responsiveness, initiation, and depth of communication to assess interest.

8. **Watch for Non-Verbal Cues:** Observe body language and eye contact in subsequent interactions for additional insights.

9. **Be Patient and Keep Perspective:** Allow the relationship to unfold naturally without rushing to conclusions.

10. **Move Forward or Step Back Appropriately:** Based on interest levels, either nurture the connection or respectfully withdraw.

Don'ts:

1. **Don't Rush to Text Immediately:** Avoid appearing overly eager or desperate by texting too soon after the date.

2. **Don't Over-analyze the Initial Text:** Avoid obsessing over the perfect wording or reading too much into the response.

3. **Don't Ignore a Lack of Response:** If you don't receive a response, stop texting; understand the signal of disinterest.

4. **Don't Force Conversations:** Don't push for engagement if responses are lukewarm or infrequent.

5. **Don't Misinterpret Politeness for Interest:** Recognize the difference between polite responses and genuine interest.

6. **Don't Overlook Communication Patterns:** Avoid ignoring signs of disinterest like minimal initiation or brief responses.

7. **Don't Neglect Non-Verbal Cues:** Avoid missing out on understanding feelings and intentions through body language.

8. **Don't Jump to Conclusions:** Avoid making assumptions about interest levels based on limited interactions.

9. **Don't Cling to Hope in Silence:** If signs point to disinterest, don't hold onto false hope; respect the situation and move on.

10. **Don't Disrespect Personal Boundaries:** If deciding to step back, do so respectfully and without bitterness.

Chapter 7

Handling Rejection and Disappointment

Part 1

Coping with Unmet Expectations

"Some of us think holding on makes us strong,
but sometimes it is letting go."

– Hermann Hesse

We all know dating unmet expectations are challenging but universally experienced. It involves navigating the complex emotions that arise when reality falls short of our hopes and desires.

The Landscape of Expectations in Dating

Expectations are a fundamental part of the dating experience. We enter the dating world filled with hopes, dreams, and desires, creating mental images of potential partners and future relationships. However, when these expectations are not met, it can lead to disappointment and self-doubt. Understanding the balance between expectation and reality and how our perceptions shape our reactions is crucial in navigating these moments.

The Emotional Response to Unmet Expectations

The initial emotional response to unmet expectations in dating can vary from mild disappointment to profound heartache. Feeling saddened or rejected when something we hoped for doesn't materialise is a natural human reaction. These emotions, while painful, are also insightful, reflecting our values, desires, and capacity for connection.

Navigating Disappointment: A Mindful Approach

Acknowledging and Accepting Emotions: The first step in coping with disappointment is recognising and accepting your feelings. Denying or suppressing emotions can lead to unhealthy manifestations. Allow yourself to feel sad, frustrated, or angry as part of the human experience.

Reframing Perspectives: After acknowledging your emotions, reframe your perspective. This doesn't mean trivialising your feelings but viewing the experience differently. Recognising that rejection is not a reflection of your worth, but rather a sign of incompatibility or differing paths can shift your understanding of the situation.

Finding Solace in Shared Experiences: You are not alone facing rejection or disappointment. Sharing your feelings with friends or hearing others' stories can provide comfort and a sense of shared humanity.

The Role of Self-Reflection

Post-disappointment is an opportune time for self-reflection. Reflect on what the experience has taught you about your desires, deal-breakers, and approach to dating. Use the situation as a learning opportunity to gain deeper insights into your dating patterns and preferences.

Moving Forward with Grace and Confidence

Moving forward after facing disappointment involves doing so with grace and confidence. Avoid letting one experience define your entire dating journey. Each interaction and disappointment is a step toward self-discovery and personal growth. Our experiences are not defined by events but by our reactions to them and the lessons we draw from them.

ooo

Sarah sat on her couch, a sense of disappointment washing over her. She had just returned from what she thought would be a promising second date with James. They had initially met at a social event and had hit it off with their shared interests and engaging conversations. Sarah couldn't help but feel excited about the possibilities.

Their first date had gone exceptionally well, and they had made plans for a second one. Sarah had imagined a future filled with more enjoyable dates, shared experiences, and growing closer to James.

However, the second date didn't go as expected. The conversation felt a bit forced, and James seemed distracted, frequently checking his phone. Sarah left the date feeling deflated, wondering where the chemistry they had initially felt had gone.

As Sarah sat with her disappointment, she acknowledged her feelings and allowed herself to experience them fully. She realised that feeling let down was a normal part of the dating journey. It reminded her that not every connection would lead to a lasting relationship, which was okay.

Sarah also recognised the importance of reframing her perspective. Instead of viewing the situation as a personal failure or rejection, she saw it as a compatibility mismatch. Their interests and communication styles didn't align, which was no one's fault.

In the following days, Sarah sought solace in talking to her friends and hearing their stories of dating disappointments. She found comfort in the shared experiences and learned she wasn't alone in facing unmet expectations.

The disappointment became an opportunity for self-reflection. Sarah thought about what she truly desired in a partner and what qualities were non-negotiable. She realised that each dating experience, even the disappointing ones, provided valuable insights into her preferences and dating patterns.

As time passed, Sarah decided to move forward with grace and confidence. She knew that one disappointing date didn't define her entire dating journey. There were more opportunities, connections, and lessons to be learned along the way.

Coping with unmet expectations was a part of the dating process, and Sarah was determined to embrace it with resilience and a positive outlook. She knew the right connection was out there, waiting to be discovered, and she was ready to continue her journey with an open heart.

ooo

Part 2

Learning from Failed Connections

"In the middle of difficulty lies opportunity."

– Albert Einstein

Continuing our exploration of dating challenges, we focus on the lessons learned from failed connections. This section delves into the rich learning opportunities that arise from relationships that don't work out as hoped.

The Nature of Failed Connections

Failed connections, whether brief dates or longer relationships that end are a part of the dating experience. They can be sources of sadness and frustration but also contain invaluable lessons. Understanding failure not as a defeat but as a source of learning and growth is particularly enlightening. Each failed connection offers insights into what works, what doesn't, and what matters most in our relationships.

Reflecting on Patterns

Reflecting on patterns in failed connections is crucial. Are there commonalities in the types of people you are drawn to or the kinds of interactions that fizzle out? Identifying these patterns can reveal unconscious behaviours or choices that may not serve you well. This reflection isn't about self-blame but about gaining clarity on your relationship dynamics.

Understanding Personal Contributions

Recognising your role in past connections is key. This involves understanding your behaviours, communication styles, and emotional responses that might have influenced the relationship's trajectory. Examining your contributions can provide a balanced and holistic view of how you engage in relationships.

Embracing Change and Growth

Failed connections are opportunities for personal growth. They can be catalysts for change, prompting us to develop new communication skills, reassess our relationship priorities, or address personal issues impacting our dating lives. These experiences can be transformative, leading to more meaningful and fulfilling relationships in the future.

The Power of Resilience

Building resilience is essential in learning from failed connections. It involves the ability to bounce back from disappointments and to approach dating with renewed hope and wisdom. It's about using past experiences to become more aware, empathetic, and open to new possibilities.

Moving Forward with New Insights

After failed connections, the lessons learned are applied to future relationships. It's about stepping into new dating experiences with a deeper understanding of yourself, more precise ideas of what you are looking for, and a refined approach to finding a compatible partner. It's the journey and the learnings along the way that enrich our lives and shape our destinies.

ooo

Michael sat alone in his favorite coffee shop, contemplating the recent end of his three-month relationship with Sarah. At first, their connection was beautiful, filled with shared laughter and common interests. However, as time passed, their differences became more apparent, leading to arguments and, ultimately, the decision to part ways.

As Michael sipped his coffee, he reflected on the lessons he had learned from this failed connection. He realised that even though it hadn't worked out, every relationship was an opportunity for growth and self-discovery.

One of the first lessons Michael gleaned was the importance of communication. In his past relationships, he had often avoided discussing complex topics to prevent conflict. This pattern repeated with Sarah, leading to unaddressed issues that eventually became insurmountable. Michael knew he needed to become more open and honest in his future relationships, tackling issues head-on instead of avoiding them.

Another lesson was about compatibility. Michael had always been attracted to outgoing and extroverted individuals like Sarah. However, he had learned that introverted partners could offer a different, equally fulfilling connection. He realised the importance of aligning values and long-term goals with a partner rather than focusing on surface-level attraction.

Michael also recognised the need for self-care and boundaries. During his relationship with Sarah, he had neglected his own needs and personal space, leading to emotional exhaustion. He understood that caring for himself was not selfish but necessary for a healthy relationship.

Embracing change and growth became a core theme in Michael's reflections. He saw the failed connection as an opportunity to become a better partner and a more self-aware individual. He decided to seek therapy to improve his communication skills and gain a deeper understanding of his emotional triggers.

Resilience was another essential lesson. Michael knew that the pain of a failed connection would fade with time, and he would emerge from it stronger and wiser. He was determined not to let this experience define his outlook on love but to use it as a stepping stone towards more meaningful and fulfilling relationships.

As Michael finished his coffee, he felt renewed hope and determination. Failed connections were not setbacks but stepping stones on his journey to find a partner who complemented him. With the lessons learned from this experience, he was ready to embrace the future with open arms and an open heart.

ooo

Do's and Don'ts

Do's:

1. **Acknowledge and Accept Emotions:** Recognize and allow yourself to feel and process your emotions after a disappointment.

2. **Reframe Perspectives:** Shift your view of the experience, seeing it as a mismatch or learning opportunity rather than a personal failure.

3. **Seek Support:** Share your feelings with friends or others who have had similar experiences for comfort and perspective.

4. **Reflect on the Experience:** Use the situation as a chance to learn about your desires, deal-breakers, and dating approach.

5. **Move Forward Gracefully:** Continue your dating journey confidently, using each experience as a step towards personal growth.

6. **Identify Patterns:** Look for common themes in your dating experiences to understand your preferences and behaviours.

7. **Recognize Your Contributions:** Understand how your actions, communication style and emotional responses may have influenced the relationship.

8. **Embrace Personal Growth:** Use failed connections as catalysts for developing new skills or addressing personal issues.

9. **Build Resilience:** Strengthen your ability to recover from disappointments and approach dating with renewed hope.

10. **Apply Lessons Learned:** Use insights from past experiences to enhance future relationships.

Don'ts:

1. **Don't Deny Your Feelings:** Avoid suppressing or ignoring your emotions, as this can lead to unhealthy coping mechanisms.

2. **Don't Dwell on Negativity:** Avoid fixating on the disappointment or viewing it as a reflection of your self-worth.

3. **Don't Isolate Yourself:** Avoid withdrawing from others; sharing your experiences can be therapeutic.

4. **Don't Repeat Unhelpful Patterns:** Avoid repeating the same dating habits without learning from past experiences.

5. **Don't Lose Confidence:** Avoid letting one experience negatively impact your self-esteem or approach to future relationships.

6. **Don't Ignore Warning Signs:** Avoid overlooking patterns that may indicate unhelpful tendencies in your dating choices.

7. **Don't Blame Yourself Exclusively.** Avoid taking full responsibility for the relationship's end; it usually involves a combination of factors.

8. **Don't Resist Change:** Avoid clinging to old habits or fears; embrace the opportunity for personal development.

9. **Don't Become Cynical:** Avoid letting disappointment make you bitter or close off to future possibilities.

10. **Don't Rush Into New Relationships:** Avoid jumping into new relationships without reflecting and learning from past experiences.

Chapter 8

The Second Date and Beyond - Deepening the Connection

Part 1

Creative Date Ideas to Foster Closeness

"Shared joy is a double joy; shared sorrow is half a sorrow."

– Swedish Proverb

Moving beyond the first date, let's delve into nurturing and deepening the connection through creative and thoughtful date ideas. This section aims to inspire unique and memorable dating experiences that strengthen the budding relationship.

The Importance of Thoughtful Planning

The choice of a date activity can significantly reflect your interest and investment in the relationship. It's not just about the activity but also about the thought that goes into planning it. The effort and creativity you put into organising a date can significantly influence the connection you're building with your partner.

Exploring Shared Interests

Building upon shared interests discovered during your initial meetings is a great starting point for planning a second date. If both of you enjoy art, visiting an art gallery or a street art tour can be delightful. If you share a love for the outdoors, a hiking adventure or a day at the beach might be ideal. These shared experiences create enjoyable moments and deepen your bond over common passions.

Trying Something New Together

Engaging in a new activity together can be an exciting way to build your connection. Trying something neither of you has done before – like a cooking class, a dance lesson, or a pottery workshop – can create a sense of adventure and playfulness in your relationship, leading to a deeper understanding and appreciation of each other.

Cultural and Educational Dates

Dates that involve cultural or educational elements, such as attending a lecture, a book reading, or a play, can provide substantial material for meaningful conversations. These experiences can stimulate intellectual compatibility and offer insights into each other's perspectives and worldviews.

Nature and Outdoors

Being in nature can be inherently bonding. Planning a date involving nature, like a picnic in a scenic park, a walk in a botanical garden, or stargazing, can provide a serene and intimate setting, fostering a sense of peace and closeness.

The Art of Dining

A traditional dinner date, with a creative twist, can transform into an extraordinary experience. Consider dining at a restaurant with a unique concept or trying a cuisine new to both. The sensory experience of tasting new flavours together can be enjoyable and memorable.

Home-Cooked Surprises

Inviting your date for a home-cooked meal shows effort, care, and a willingness to open up your personal space. Cooking together can be a fun and intimate activity, providing opportunities for collaboration and sharing personal stories.

Reflective and Quiet Dates

Meaningful connections are often fostered in quiet, reflective settings. A date that involves visiting a museum, a quiet café, or even just a walk in a tranquil area can provide space for deeper, introspective conversations.

ooo

Sarah and Alex had been on a few dates and were eager to explore new and creative ways to deepen their connection. They both shared a love for the arts, so they decided to plan a date that would allow them to explore their creative sides.

They started their day by visiting a local art gallery. They wandered through the exhibits, taking time to appreciate the diverse artworks. Sarah was drawn to abstract paintings, while Alex had a keen interest in photography. They shared their thoughts and interpretations of the art, leading to insightful discussions about their personal perspectives and artistic preferences.

After the gallery visit, they headed to a nearby park for a picnic. Sarah had prepared a basket of delicious sandwiches, fresh fruit, and homemade lemonade. They laid a blanket under a shady tree and enjoyed eating while watching the ducks in the nearby pond. The serene natural setting allowed them to relax and connect deeper.

Next on their agenda was a pottery workshop. Neither of them had ever tried pottery before, making it a perfect opportunity for a new experience together. They sat side by side at the pottery wheel, getting their hands dirty as they shaped clay into unique creations. It was a playful and slightly messy adventure that brought out their creativity and laughter.

To cap off their day, they had dinner at a charming restaurant tucked away in a quiet neighborhood. The restaurant had a cosy atmosphere and served cuisine from a region neither of them had explored before. They shared dishes and savoured the flavours, discussing their day's highlights and hopes for the future.

Finally, they decided to end their date with a touch of magic. They drove to a secluded spot outside the city where the night sky was clear and filled with stars. They lay on a blanket, holding hands, and gazed up at the constellations. In the quiet darkness, they shared their dreams and aspirations, feeling a profound sense of connection under the vast expanse of the universe.

As Sarah and Alex headed home, they both felt a sense of warmth and closeness that deepened throughout their creative and thoughtful date. They realised that nurturing their connection through shared experiences and meaningful conversations was a beautiful way to foster a strong and lasting relationship.

ooo

Part 2

Navigating Early Relationship Challenges

"The course of true love never did run smooth."

– William Shakespeare

As we venture further into the journey of a budding relationship, we encounter the inevitable challenges of early dating. This section delves into understanding and overcoming the hurdles that often arise as a relationship starts to deepen.

Understanding the Natural Progression of Relationships

The early stages of a relationship can be exhilarating but also bring various uncertainties and challenges.

Recognising these as natural parts of the relationship's growth is crucial for maintaining perspective and patience. Understanding the context and progression of the relationship is key to navigating these early stages.

Communication: The Bedrock of Resolution

Address Misunderstandings Early: Misunderstandings naturally arise when partners are still getting to know each other. The best way to handle them is through open, honest communication. By creating an environment where both people can freely express thoughts and emotions, misunderstandings can be clarified and resolved before they escalate.

Balance Expectations with Reality: Each person enters a relationship carrying their own hopes and assumptions. Problems surface when these expectations clash with real-life circumstances. Discussing your expectations openly and being willing to adapt as the relationship progresses is essential for maintaining harmony.

Navigating Differences

Respecting Individuality: Balancing the excitement of romance with the need to maintain individuality is a common challenge. Appreciating and embracing each other's differences is essential, as they contribute to what makes each person unique.

Finding Common Ground: While respecting differences, finding common ground in shared values, interests, and goals can strengthen the bond and provide a foundation for the relationship.

The Role of Compromise

Compromise is essential, especially in the early stages of a relationship. It involves finding a balance where both partners feel their needs and desires are respected. Reconciling differing viewpoints is a key aspect of navigating early relationship challenges.

Dealing with External Influences

Handling External Pressures: External pressures, such as opinions from friends and family or societal expectations, can pose challenges. Maintaining a united front and discussing how to handle these pressures is important.

Balancing Relationship with Other Life Aspects: It can be challenging to balance the excitement of a new relationship with other life responsibilities. Effective time management and clear communication about priorities can help maintain this balance.

Embracing Vulnerability

Vulnerability is a powerful tool in deepening connections. Being open about fears, insecurities, and hopes can strengthen trust and understanding between partners. Embracing vulnerability paves the way for deeper emotional intimacy.

Growing Together Through Challenges

Early relationship challenges are not roadblocks but stepping stones toward a stronger and more meaningful connection. Navigating these challenges requires patience, understanding, effective communication, and a willingness to grow together. Each challenge offers an opportunity to deepen the bond and understanding between partners.

ooo

Sarah and Alex had been dating for a few months, and their relationship was evolving. They had moved past the initial excitement of their first few dates and were now faced with the realities and challenges of building a deeper connection.

One evening, after a minor disagreement about weekend plans, they decided to have an open conversation. They both recognised that misunderstandings were bound to happen and addressing them with honesty and empathy was the key to resolving conflicts. They discussed their individual expectations for the weekend and found a compromise that made them happy. This discussion reinforced the importance of communication in their relationship.

As the weeks passed, Sarah and Alex began noticing their differences more prominently. Sarah was a morning person, while Alex was a night owl. They also had varying tastes in music and hobbies. Rather than letting these differences create distance, they decided to embrace them. They enjoyed introducing each other to their favorite music genres and exploring new hobbies together. This brought them closer and allowed them to appreciate each other's unique qualities.

Compromise played a significant role in their relationship. They encountered situations where their individual desires clashed, but they always made an effort to find a middle ground. Whether deciding on the restaurant for dinner or making weekend plans, they learned that making small sacrifices for each other's happiness was a fundamental part of growing together.

External influences also tested their relationship. Sarah's friends had differing opinions about Alex, and Alex's family had their own set of expectations. Instead of letting these external pressures create tension, Sarah and Alex discussed how to handle them. They decided to maintain open communication and present a united front to address any concerns from friends and family. This approach strengthened their bond and helped them navigate the external challenges together.

Vulnerability became a cornerstone of their relationship. They realised that sharing their fears, insecurities, and hopes brought them closer. Opening up about their past experiences and emotional scars allowed them to build trust and deepen their emotional intimacy.

In the end, Sarah and Alex understood that early relationship challenges were not obstacles but opportunities for growth. They embraced these challenges with patience, empathy, and effective communication. Each challenge they faced allowed them to grow together, strengthening their connection and making their relationship more meaningful. They learned that the journey of love was not always smooth, but the challenges along the way enriched their bond and brought them closer together.

Do's and Don'ts

Do's:

1. **Plan Thoughtfully:** Show your interest and investment in the relationship by thoughtfully planning dates that reflect shared interests or new experiences.

2. **Explore Shared Interests:** Build upon common passions or hobbies discovered during initial meetings to create enjoyable and bonding experiences.

3. **Try New Activities Together:** Engage in new and exciting activities to add adventure and playfulness to your relationship.

4. **Incorporate Cultural and Educational Elements:** Choose dates that stimulate intellectual compatibility and offer insights into each other's perspectives.

5. **Enjoy Nature Together:** Use nature's serene and intimate setting to foster closeness and peace in your relationship.

6. **Be Creative with Dining:** Transform a traditional dinner date by trying unique cuisines or dining concepts.

7. **Invite for Home-Cooked Meals:** Show care and openness by inviting your date for a meal you've prepared, creating an intimate and collaborative experience.

8. **Embrace Quiet, Reflective Dates:** Choose settings that allow for deeper, introspective conversations.

9. **Communicate Effectively:** Address misunderstandings and balance expectations with reality through open and honest communication.

10. **Respect Individuality:** Embrace and respect each other's differences while finding common ground in shared values and goals.

11. **Practice Compromise:** Find balance in the relationship by compromising and reconciling differing viewpoints.

12. **Handle External Pressures Together:** Discuss and manage external influences as a united team.

13. **Balance Relationship with Other Life Aspects:** Effectively manage time to balance your relationship and other responsibilities.

14. **Be Vulnerable:** Share your fears, insecurities, and hopes to build trust and deepen emotional intimacy.

Don'ts:

1. **Don't Neglect Planning:** Avoid showing a lack of effort or interest by not planning dates thoughtfully.

2. **Don't Ignore Shared Interests:** Avoid missing opportunities to bond over common hobbies or passions.

3. **Don't Stick to Routine Activities:** Avoid falling into a monotonous pattern by not trying new things together.

4. **Don't Overlook Intellectual Compatibility:** Avoid missing out on deep conversations and connections by not engaging in cultural or educational activities.

5. **Don't Dismiss the Power of Nature:** Avoid overlooking the bonding effect of spending time in natural settings.

6. **Don't Settle for Ordinary Dining Experiences:** Avoid missing the chance to create memorable

experiences by sticking to conventional dining options.

7.   **Don't Hesitate to Open Your Space:** Avoid missing an opportunity for intimacy by not inviting your date for a home-cooked meal.

8.   **Don't Avoid Deep Conversations:** Avoid superficiality by not engaging in reflective and meaningful discussions.

9.   **Don't Miscommunicate:** Avoid misunderstandings and conflicts by not communicating openly and honestly.

10. **Don't Disregard Each Other's Individuality:** Avoid creating tension by not respecting and embracing differences.

11. **Don't Refuse to Compromise:** Avoid conflicts and resentment by not being willing to find a middle ground.

12. **Don't Let External Influences Overwhelm:** Avoid allowing outside opinions or pressures to impact your relationship negatively.

13. **Don't Neglect Other Aspects of Life:** Avoid imbalance by not managing your time effectively between your relationship and other responsibilities.

14. **Don't Close Off Emotionally:** Avoid hindering emotional intimacy by not being open and vulnerable with your partner.

Chapter 9

From Casual to Serious
– The Transition Phase

Part 1

Recognizing the Shift: When Casual Becomes Committed

"Growth is the only evidence of life."

– John Henry Newman

Now is the time to explore the subtle yet significant transition from casual dating to a more serious, committed relationship. Focus on identifying and understanding the signs and nuances of this crucial phase.

The Evolution of a Relationship

Relationships are dynamic and evolve over time. The transition from casual to serious is often marked not by grand gestures or explicit declarations but by subtle shifts in interaction, feelings, and expectations. It's a process in which small, seemingly inconsequential details gradually weave together to form a more profound picture.

The Signs of Deepening Connection

Increased Time Spent Together: A natural increase in the time spent together is one of the first signs of a relationship becoming more serious. It's a shift from planning dates to a desire to share more aspects of your lives with each other.

Deepening Emotional Intimacy: As the relationship deepens, so does emotional intimacy. Conversations move beyond surface-level topics and delve into personal and vulnerable areas, indicating a strengthening bond.

Integration into Each Other's Lives: Gradually, you start to become a part of each other's social circles and routines. Introduction to friends and family and participation in each other's important events are indicators of the relationship's growing significance.

Consistency and Reliability: With a more serious relationship, the erratic uncertainty of casual dating starts to wane. There's a consistency in communication and plans and a growing reliance on each other.

The Shift in Priorities

A shift in priorities is a telling sign that a relationship has moved from casual to serious. Your partner becomes a significant consideration in your decision-making process, reflecting a view of things through the lens of a partnership.

Mutual Growth and Support

The transition also involves evolving from individual growth to mutual growth. Supporting and encouraging each other's personal development and facing challenges together indicate a deeper connection.

Feeling the Change

The shift from casual to serious is often felt more than explicitly discussed initially. A sense of comfort, security, and mutual respect permeates the relationship, marked by subtleties and underlying changes in dynamics.

Embracing the Transition

Recognising the shift from casual to serious involves being attentive to the subtle changes in the relationship's dynamics. It's about noticing the deepening connection, integration into each other's lives, consistency, reliability, and evolving priorities. Understanding this transition phase requires a keen awareness of the evolving nature of your relationship.

ooo

Karen and Mark had been dating for several months, and their relationship gradually evolved from casual to more committed. Neither had explicitly discussed the shift, but they could feel it deepening their connection.

One of the first signs they noticed was their increased time together. What started as occasional dates had turned into spending weekends together and sharing weekday evenings. It felt natural to want to be around each other more often.

Their conversations had also evolved. They found themselves discussing more personal and vulnerable topics. Karen opened up about her dreams and fears, and Mark shared his past experiences. They felt a growing emotional intimacy, a sense of trust that allowed them to be their authentic selves.

Integration into each other's lives was another significant indicator. Mark introduced Karen to his close friends, and Karen invited Mark to family gatherings. They were becoming more involved in each other's social circles, and it felt like a natural progression.

Consistency and reliability had replaced the uncertainty of casual dating. They no longer had to play the "waiting game" or wonder if the other person was interested. Texts and calls were more frequent, and plans were made with confidence.

A noticeable shift in priorities had also occurred. They began considering each other when making decisions about their future. Karen's career plans started to include the possibility of moving closer to Mark, and Mark began factoring Karen into his long-term goals. It was no longer just about "me" but "us."

Mutual growth and support had become integral to their relationship. They encouraged each other's personal development, whether pursuing new career opportunities or working on self-improvement. They faced challenges together, knowing they had a partner to rely on.

But perhaps the shift's most significant sign was how they felt. Their relationship was characterised by a deep sense of comfort, security, and mutual respect. They didn't need to discuss becoming more serious because they both knew it.

Karen and Mark's story illustrates the natural progression from casual dating to a committed relationship. This transition is marked by subtle changes in dynamics, increased time together, deepening emotional intimacy, integration into each other's lives, consistency, shifting priorities, mutual growth, and, above all, a profound feeling that something special is happening. Recognising this shift requires being attuned to the evolving nature of their relationship and embracing the journey ahead.

ooo

Part 2

Communicating About Exclusivity

"Love is a commitment to protecting another person's heart with the same passion you use to guard your own."

– Rob Hill Sr.

Sooner or later, we reach the pivotal moment of discussing exclusivity in a relationship. This phase, rich in significance and potential apprehension, involves navigating this delicate topic with sensitivity, openness, and honesty.

The Timing of the Conversation

One of the most challenging aspects of discussing exclusivity is deciding when to have the conversation. Timing can be crucial in relationships, just as in many other aspects of life. It's generally advisable to wait until there is a mutual depth of feeling and commitment. If signs of a serious relationship are consistently present, it might be the right time to discuss the nature of your relationship.

Approaching the Topic

Setting the Scene: Choose a comfortable and private setting for the discussion, where both of you feel comfortable expressing your thoughts and feelings openly.

Expressing Your Feelings: Start by sharing your feelings about the relationship and why you feel ready to take it to the next level. Be honest and clear about your emotions and be prepared to listen.

Listening and Understanding: After expressing your viewpoint, allow your partner to share theirs. Listen actively, without judgment or interruption, to understand their feelings and concerns.

Handling Different Perspectives

If your partner is not ready for exclusivity or has a different view of the relationship from yours, handle these differences with respect and understanding. Avoid pressuring or convincing; instead, focus on understanding their perspective and expressing yourself honestly.

Communicating Expectations

If both parties agree to become exclusive, it's important to communicate your expectations moving forward. Discuss what exclusivity means to each of you and address any specific boundaries or considerations. Breaking down what exclusivity means in practical terms can prevent misunderstandings later on.

Respecting the Process

Regardless of the outcome, respect the process and the conversation. If your partner needs time to consider exclusivity, give them that space. If you decide to remain non-exclusive, consider what this means for your relationship moving forward.

Building on Open Communication

Concluding the conversation about exclusivity reinforces open and honest communication as the foundation of your relationship. Whether it leads to exclusivity or not, this conversation should strengthen your ability to communicate and understand each other.

ooo

Lena and James had been dating for several months, and their connection had grown stronger with each passing day. They both felt that their relationship was moving in a meaningful direction, and the time had come to discuss exclusivity.

Choosing the right timing for the conversation was essential. They wanted to make sure it wasn't too early, as they didn't want to rush into anything, but they also didn't want to wait too long, as the topic was important to both of them.

They decided on a cosy evening at Lena's place as the setting for the conversation. It was a comfortable and private space where they could share their thoughts openly. They began the discussion by expressing their feelings for each other.

Lena spoke first, explaining how much she had enjoyed their time together and felt a deep connection with James. She shared her desire to take their relationship to the next level and explore exclusivity.

James listened attentively and appreciated Lena's honesty. He expressed his feelings, which mirrored Lena's. He admitted that he had been thinking about exclusivity, too, and was glad Lena had brought it up.

As they continued talking, they realised they were on the same page. Both wanted to be exclusive and commit to each other. They discussed what exclusivity meant to each of them, agreeing that it involved focusing on their relationship and not dating other people.

They also communicated their expectations about spending more time together, introducing each other to their respective social circles, and supporting each other's personal growth.

However, not all conversations about exclusivity end with such a mutual agreement. Lena and James understood that one person could have a different perspective. They had both agreed that if that were the case, they would respect each other's feelings and decisions.

In the end, their conversation about exclusivity strengthened their bond. They felt even more connected, knowing they had communicated openly and honestly about their desires and intentions. It was a significant step in their relationship, built on a foundation of trust and understanding.

Lena and James' story highlights the importance of approaching the topic of exclusivity with sensitivity, openness, and honesty. It's about choosing the right timing, expressing feelings, listening to each other, and respecting different perspectives. Whether the outcome is exclusivity or not, the conversation should reinforce the importance of open communication in the relationship.

ooo

Do's and Don'ts

Do's:

1. **Recognize Relationship Evolution:** Be attentive to subtle shifts in interaction and feelings, indicating a move towards a more serious relationship.

2. **Identify Signs of Deepening Connection:** Look for increased time spent together, deeper emotional intimacy, and integration into each other's lives as signs of a growing bond.

3. **Choose the Right Time for Exclusivity Talk:** Wait to discuss exclusivity until there is a mutual depth of feeling and commitment.

4. **Set a Comfortable Scene for Discussion:** Choose a private, relaxed setting for the exclusivity conversation.

5. **Express Your Feelings Clearly:** Share your emotions and reasons for wanting to take the relationship to the next level.

6. **Listen Actively to Your Partner:** Give your partner space to express their feelings and listen without judgment.

7. **Handle Differences Respectfully:** If views on exclusivity differ, respect your partner's perspective and avoid pressuring them.

8. **Communicate Expectations Clearly:** If moving towards exclusivity, discuss what it means for both of you and set clear boundaries.

9. **Respect the Process:** Honor the conversation, whether it leads to exclusivity or not, and use it to strengthen your communication skills.

Don'ts:

1. **Don't Ignore Relationship Changes:** Avoid overlooking the signs that indicate your relationship is becoming more serious.

2. **Don't Rush the Exclusivity Conversation:** Avoid bringing up exclusivity too early or without sensing a mutual depth in the relationship.

3. **Don't Choose an Inappropriate Setting:** Avoid discussing exclusivity in public or uncomfortable settings.

4. **Don't Be Vague About Your Feelings.** Avoid ambiguity and be clear about your feelings and desires for the relationship.

5. **Don't Dismiss Your Partner's Perspective:** During the exclusivity talk, avoid ignoring or minimizing your partner's feelings.

6. **Don't Pressure for Exclusivity:** Avoid forcing the idea of exclusivity if your partner is not ready or willing.

7. **Don't Leave Expectations Undefined:** Avoid vagueness about what exclusivity means to avoid future misunderstandings.

8. **Don't Disrespect Your Partner's Decision:** If your partner needs time or decides against exclusivity, respect their choice.

9. **Don't Neglect Communication:** Avoid letting the outcome of the exclusivity talk hinder ongoing open and honest communication in your relationship.

Chapter 10

Maintaining a Healthy Relationship

Part 1

Balancing Independence with Intimacy

"Without freedom, there is no creation."

– Jiddu Krishnamurti

It is critical to explore the delicate balance between maintaining individual independence and nurturing intimacy in a relationship. This balance involves a harmonious blend of autonomy and interconnectedness.

The Interplay of Independence and Intimacy

A healthy relationship requires a balance of independence and intimacy. While intimacy involves sharing one's life with another, independence emphasises maintaining one's sense of self within the relationship. Finding a balance that respects both the need for personal space and the desire for close connection is crucial.

Fostering Individuality

Personal Interests and Hobbies: Encouraging each other to pursue personal interests and hobbies is crucial for nurturing individual growth and bringing new energy into the relationship.

Time Apart: Spending time apart is a sign of a healthy relationship. It allows for personal reflection, growth, and the maintenance of individual identities, providing fresh perspectives and appreciation for each other.

Building Intimacy

Quality Time Together: Investing in quality time together is crucial for building intimacy. Finding meaningfulness in everyday moments strengthens the connection.

Deep Communication: Regular, deep communication is the cornerstone of intimacy. It involves sharing thoughts, feelings, fears, and joys with your partner and being vulnerable and open with them.

Navigating the Tension

The tension between independence and intimacy is natural. Navigating it requires ongoing communication and adjustment. Regular check-ins about each partner's feelings regarding the balance can be helpful.

Respecting Differences

Each person has a unique comfort level with independence and intimacy. Respecting these differences is key. It's about understanding and honoring your partner's needs for space or closeness, even if they differ from yours.

The Role of Trust

Trust is at the heart of balancing independence and intimacy. Building trust involves consistency, reliability, and open communication, allowing for autonomy without insecurity and emotional vulnerability.

A Dynamic Equilibrium

Maintaining a healthy relationship involves finding a dynamic equilibrium between independence and intimacy. It's a continuous process of communication, understanding, and adjustment, striving for harmony that fosters individual growth and deep connection.

ooo

Sophie and Mark had been in a relationship for two years, and they cherished the deep connection they had built. However, they also recognised the importance of maintaining individual independence within the relationship.

Fostering individuality was a priority for both of them. They encouraged each other to pursue their personal interests and hobbies. Sophie, a passionate photographer, often spent weekends on photography trips, while Mark enjoyed hiking with his friends. They understood that these activities brought them joy and enriched their relationship by giving them new experiences and stories to share.

Another aspect they valued was time apart. They had a standing agreement that each would have one evening a week for personal reflection and activities. This time allowed them to maintain their sense of self and return to the relationship with a fresh perspective.

Building intimacy was equally important to Sophie and Mark. They dedicated quality time to each other, ensuring that their moments together were meaningful. Whether it was cooking a meal together, going for long walks, or simply cuddling on the couch, they cherished these moments of togetherness.

Communication was at the heart of their relationship. Sophie and Mark regularly engaged in deep conversations. They shared their thoughts, feelings, fears, and joys openly, creating an environment of trust and vulnerability. This open communication strengthened their emotional connection and allowed them to better understand each other.

Of course, there were moments of tension between their desire for independence and their need for intimacy. They found regular check-ins about how they felt about the balance helpful. They would openly discuss whether they needed more alone time or extra quality time together.

Importantly, Sophie and Mark respected each other's differences. They understood that they had unique comfort levels with independence and intimacy. Mark appreciated Sophie's need for occasional solitude, and Sophie admired Mark's ability to nurture close connections with his friends.

Trust played a central role in their relationship. They trusted each other's commitment to maintaining the balance between independence and intimacy. Their consistency, reliability, and open communication allowed them to enjoy their independence without insecurity.

Sophie and Mark's story illustrates the delicate balance between independence and intimacy in a relationship. They found a dynamic equilibrium by fostering individuality, building intimacy through quality time and communication, and navigating the tension with respect and trust. Their relationship was a harmonious blend of personal growth and deep connection, a testament to the importance of balance in love.

ooo

Do's and Don'ts

Do's:

1. **Encourage Personal Interests:** Support each other in pursuing individual hobbies and interests.

2. **Value Time Apart:** Recognize the importance of spending time apart for personal growth and maintaining individual identities.

3. **Invest in Quality Time Together:** Prioritize meaningful activities and moments together to strengthen your bond.

4. **Foster Deep Communication:** Share thoughts, feelings, and vulnerabilities openly to build emotional intimacy.

5. **Respect Individual Differences:** Acknowledge and embrace each other's unique needs for space or closeness.

6. **Build Trust:** Develop consistency and reliability in your actions and communication to foster independence without insecurity.

Don'ts:

1. **Neglect Personal Growth:** Avoid becoming so intertwined that you lose sight of your individual growth and interests.

2. **Overlook the Need for Alone Time:** Don't underestimate the importance of solitude and personal reflection in a relationship.

3. **Ignore Communication:** Avoid letting conversations remain superficial; delve into deeper, more meaningful discussions.

4. **Disrespect Boundaries:** Don't push your partner to spend all their time with you or vice versa; respect their need for independence.

5. **Assume One-Size-Fits-All:** Avoid imposing your own balance of independence and intimacy onto your partner without considering their comfort level.

Part 2

Continuous Growth and Adaptation

"Love is not a state of perfect caring.
It is an active noun, like struggle."

– Fred Rogers

How about continuous growth and adaptation in relationships? Recognising that relationships, like individuals, evolve over time is crucial for their longevity and depends on the couple's ability to grow and adapt together.

Embracing Change as a Constant

Change is a constant in life, and in the context of a relationship, this means accepting that both you and your partner will evolve over time. Embracing these changes, rather than resisting them, is key to a healthy and enduring relationship. It's about supporting each other through different life stages, career transitions, and personal transformations.

The Art of Adaptation

Adaptation in a relationship involves proactively creating an environment where both partners can thrive. This includes:

Open Communication: Maintaining open lines of communication is crucial for understanding each other's evolving needs and expectations. Honest conversations about feelings, aspirations, and concerns help us navigate changes together.

Flexibility: Flexibility and open-mindedness help people adapt to changes. This might mean redefining roles, adjusting plans and goals, or more accommodating each other's needs.

Compromise: It is essential to compromise where both partners feel their needs are met. The compromise should respect both partners' needs and boundaries.

Cultivating Shared Goals and Values

Fostering shared goals and values can strengthen the bond between partners. Setting common objectives related to lifestyle, career, family, or personal growth creates a sense of unity and purpose.

The Importance of Emotional Intelligence

Developing emotional intelligence is vital for a relationship's growth and adaptation. It helps you effectively navigate conflicts, understand and respond to your partner's emotional needs, and maintain a healthy emotional connection.

Nurturing a Growth Mindset

Approaching the relationship with a growth mindset can be transformative. This involves viewing challenges and conflicts as opportunities for growth, being open to feedback, and continuously striving to improve as individuals and partners.

Celebrating Milestones and Creating New Experiences

Celebrating milestones reinforces the sense of shared journey and achievement. Creating new experiences together – like travelling, pursuing a shared hobby, or undertaking a joint project – can bring fresh energy and novelty into the relationship.

An Evolving Partnership

Maintaining a healthy relationship involves embracing continuous growth and adaptation. Relationships can flourish and endure over the years by nurturing a dynamic where change is welcomed, communication is open, and growth is pursued.

ooo

Emily and David had been together for ten years, and their love story was a testament to the power of continuous growth and adaptation in a relationship.

They understood that change was a constant in life and that it was essential to embrace it. Over the years, they had seen each other evolve in various ways – from career changes to personal growth and even changes in their interests and hobbies. Instead of resisting these changes, they celebrated them. They recognised that growth was a sign of a healthy individual and, by extension, a healthy relationship.

The art of adaptation played a significant role in their journey. Open communication was at the forefront of their relationship. They made it a habit to have honest conversations about their feelings, aspirations, and concerns. When they faced life-altering decisions, such as relocating for a new job or considering starting a family, they approached these changes as a team. They were flexible in their roles and were always willing to adjust plans and goals to accommodate each other's evolving needs.

Compromise was another cornerstone of their relationship. They understood that finding common ground was essential. They respected each other's boundaries while ensuring that both felt their needs were met. Over the years, they had mastered this delicate balancing act.

Emily and David had cultivated shared goals and values that strengthened their bond. They set common objectives related to their lifestyle, career aspirations, and family plans. These shared goals gave them a sense of unity and purpose, a shared path they walked together.

Emotional intelligence was another area where they excelled. They had developed the ability to navigate conflicts effectively, understand each other's emotional needs, and maintain a deep emotional connection. This emotional intelligence allowed them to weather storms and emerge more potent as a couple.

They approached their relationship with a growth mindset, seeing challenges and conflicts as opportunities for personal and collective growth. They were open to feedback, continuously worked on improving themselves, and encouraged each other to pursue personal growth goals.

Emily and David celebrated milestones together, from anniversaries to personal achievements. These celebrations reminded them of their shared journey and the love they had built over the years. They also made it a point to create new experiences together, whether travelling to a new destination, learning a new hobby, or taking on a joint project. These experiences brought fresh energy and novelty into their relationship, keeping it vibrant and exciting.

Emily and David's love story is a testament to the power of continuous growth and adaptation in a relationship. By embracing change, nurturing open communication, fostering shared goals and values, and maintaining a growth mindset, they have built a relationship that has not only endured but thrived over the years. Theirs is a love that continues to evolve, an evolving partnership that grows stronger each day.

ooo

Do's and Don'ts

Do's:

1. **Embrace Change:** Welcome personal and relational changes as opportunities for growth.

2. **Maintain Open Communication:** Keep lines of communication open to understand evolving needs and expectations.

3. **Be Flexible:** Show willingness to adapt to changes in your relationship and each other's lives.

4. **Compromise Effectively:** Find a balance that respects both partners' needs and boundaries.

5. **Set Shared Goals:** Work on common objectives to strengthen your bond.

6. **Develop Emotional Intelligence:** Cultivate the ability to understand and respond to each other's emotional needs.

7. **Celebrate Milestones:** Acknowledge and celebrate significant moments and achievements together.

8. **Create New Experiences:** Regularly engage in new activities to bring fresh energy into the relationship.

Don'ts:

1. **Resist Change:** Avoid clinging to the status quo; be open to evolving as individuals and as a couple.

2. **Close-Off Communication:** Don't shut down or avoid discussing changes or challenges in your relationship.

3. **Remain Inflexible:** Avoid being rigid in your expectations or unwilling to adapt to new circumstances.

4. **Neglect Compromise:** Don't overlook the importance of finding a middle ground in disagreements.

5. **Ignore Shared Values:** Avoid losing sight of common goals and values that bring you together.

6. **Dismiss Emotional Needs:** Don't ignore or downplay your partner's emotional expressions or needs.

7. **Overlook Celebrations:** Avoid taking milestones for granted; these are opportunities to strengthen your bond.

8. **Stagnate in Routine:** Don't let your relationship fall into monotony; actively seek new experiences to keep it vibrant.

Chapter 11

Long-Term Commitment - Making It Last

Part 1

Understanding the Dynamics of Long-Term Relationships

"The best love is the kind that awakens the soul and makes us reach for more."

– Nicholas Sparks

Long-term relationships can be both intricate and deeply fulfilling, hinging on the essential dynamics that sustain their resilience and well-being.

The Evolution of a Long-Term Relationship

Long-term relationships evolve through various stages, beginning with the thrill of discovery and gradually moving into more profound understanding and commitment. It is important to recognize that this evolution is natural and necessary, as change and adaptation are vital to the growth and success of any relationship.

Nurturing Deep Emotional Connections

Continuous Emotional Investment: Continually nurturing the emotional bond is crucial in a long-term relationship. This involves consistently connecting, understanding, and empathising with your partner, celebrating their joys, supporting them through challenges, and being a constant source of love and encouragement.

Communication as a Lifeline: Effective communication remains essential. It involves regular check-ins, sharing thoughts and feelings, and addressing issues before they escalate.

Balancing Familiarity and Novelty

Balancing the comfort of familiarity with the excitement of novelty is challenging in long-term relationships. Keeping the relationship dynamic involves creating new experiences and learning and growing together.

The Role of Mutual Respect and Appreciation

Respect and appreciation are cornerstones of a healthy long-term relationship. Valuing your partner for who they are, acknowledging their qualities, and expressing gratitude maintain a positive and loving atmosphere.

Managing Conflicts Constructively

Conflict management is crucial in long-term relationships. Constructive conflict management involves listening to understand, avoiding blame, and seeking compromise, focusing on problem-solving rather than assigning fault.

The Importance of Individual Growth

Individual growth is just as significant as the growth of the relationship. Encouraging each other to pursue personal goals, interests, and self-improvement contributes significantly to the success and happiness of the relationship.

The Continuous Journey

Navigating the dynamics of long-term relationships is a continuous journey involving deep emotional investment, effective communication, balancing familiarity with novelty, mutual respect, constructive conflict management, and supporting individual growth. The journey of a long-term relationship, rich with learning, growth, and profound connection, unfolds over time, offering deeper insights and a stronger bond.

ooo

Sarah and John had been together for over two decades, a testament to the intricate dynamics of long-term relationships. Their story was a dance of love, filled with highs and lows but always moving forward.

Their journey began with the excitement of discovery, and their hearts raced with the thrill of a new romance. But they soon realised that love was not just about the initial spark but a slow burn that required continuous effort and emotional investment.

Nurturing their deep emotional connection had become second nature. They celebrated each other's joys, offering unwavering support and encouragement. They knew that being there for one another through life's challenges was essential to their commitment.

Communication was their lifeline. They had learned that talking openly and honestly about their thoughts and feelings was the key to understanding each other. They had regular check-ins to discuss problems and share their dreams and aspirations, ensuring that they were always on the same page.

Balancing familiarity with novelty was a delicate act they had perfected over the years. They cherished their routines but also made a point to create new experiences together. From travelling to new destinations to learning new hobbies, they kept the spark alive by embracing the excitement of the unknown.

Respect and appreciation were the foundation of their relationship. They valued each other for who they were and their quirks and expressed their gratitude daily. The little things mattered – a loving note, a surprise dinner, or a heartfelt compliment.

Conflict was not a threat but an opportunity for growth. They had mastered the art of constructive conflict management. They listened to understand, avoided blame, and focused on finding solutions together. They knew it was okay to disagree; how they resolved their differences mattered.

Individual growth was encouraged and celebrated. They supported each other's personal goals, interests, and self-improvement journeys. They believed a strong relationship was built on two strong individuals who continued growing together.

Sarah and John's story was a beautiful testament to the dynamics of long-term relationships. They understood that love was not static; it was a continuous journey of deep emotional investment, effective communication, balance between familiarity and novelty, mutual respect, constructive conflict management, and individual growth. Their dance of love was a timeless journey filled with learning, growth, and an enduring affection that only grew stronger with time.

ooo

Do's and Don'ts

Do's:

1. **Embrace Relationship Evolution:** Recognize and accept that long-term relationships will evolve and change over time.

2. **Nurture Emotional Connections:** Continuously invest in deepening the emotional bond through understanding, empathy, and shared experiences.

3. **Communicate Effectively:** Maintain open and honest communication, regularly addressing issues and sharing feelings.

4. **Balance Familiarity and Novelty:** Keep the relationship dynamic by introducing new experiences and maintaining excitement.

5. **Show Respect and Appreciation:** Regularly express gratitude and respect for your partner, valuing their contributions to the relationship.

6. **Manage Conflicts Constructively:** Approach conflicts with a problem-solving mindset, focusing on understanding and resolution.

7. **Support Individual Growth:** Encourage and support each other's personal goals and interests outside the relationship.

Don'ts:

1. **Resist Change:** Avoid clinging to how the relationship used to be; be open to growth and new phases.

2. **Neglect Emotional Investment:** Don't take the emotional connection for granted; it needs continual nurturing.

3. **Let Communication Falter:** Avoid assuming your partner knows your feelings or needs without expressing them.

4. **Stagnate in Routine:** Don't let the relationship become monotonous; actively seek new experiences together.

5. **Take Your Partner for Granted:** Avoid overlooking the importance of appreciation and respect in maintaining a healthy relationship.

6. **Handle Conflicts Destructively:** Don't let conflicts escalate without resolution or resort to blame and criticism.

7. **Suppress Individuality:** Don't discourage your partner from pursuing their own interests and personal growth.

ooo

Part 2

Preparing for a Lifelong Partnership

"A successful marriage requires falling in love many times, always with the same person."

– Mignon McLaughlin

How do we prepare for a lifelong partnership, and what are the key aspects of fostering and maintaining a long-lasting romantic relationship?

Building a Foundation of Trust and Commitment

A lifelong partnership is anchored in trust and commitment. It involves consistently choosing each other through life's ups and downs. This foundational trust is built over time through shared experiences and challenges that are overcome together, continuously reaffirming the commitment to each other.

The Importance of Shared Values and Goals

Aligning core values and life goals is crucial in a lifelong partnership. These shared values and goals act as a compass, guiding the couple's journey together and providing a mutual understanding of what is important to each person and what you both aim to achieve in life.

Cultivating Emotional and Physical Intimacy

Long-term relationships thrive on sustained emotional and physical intimacy. Keeping the emotional connection alive involves continuous, open, honest communication, emotional support, and vulnerability. Physical intimacy also remains essential, requiring prioritisation and nurturing.

Embracing Change and Growing Together

Change is inevitable in any long-term commitment. Embracing change and adapting to new circumstances is crucial in lifelong partnerships. It's about growing together, supporting each other through personal and professional changes, and being flexible and understanding as life evolves.

Maintaining Individual Identities

Maintaining individual identities is essential in a deep union. Supporting each other's interests, friendships, and pursuits outside of the relationship enriches the partnership and contributes to personal growth and fulfilment.

The Art of Conflict Resolution

Conflict resolution is key in a lifelong partnership. It involves active listening, empathy, avoiding blame, finding mutually satisfying solutions, and approaching conflicts as a team to strengthen the relationship.

Continual Investment in the Relationship

A lifelong partnership requires continual investment. Regularly taking the time to connect, communicate, and show appreciation for each other is crucial. It's about never taking the relationship for granted and always striving to keep the connection strong, vibrant, and evolving.

A Journey of Enduring Partnership

Preparing for a lifelong partnership involves building trust, aligning values, maintaining intimacy, embracing change, preserving individuality, resolving conflicts constructively, and continually investing in the relationship. A successful lifelong partnership requires depth, understanding, and ongoing effort, like the layers contributing to lasting success in various realms.

ooo

Emily and Daniel had been together for what felt like a lifetime, and their relationship was a testament to the preparation and commitment required for a lifelong partnership. Their journey had been marked by trust, shared values, emotional and physical intimacy, adaptability, individuality, effective conflict resolution, and continuous investment in their love story.

Trust and commitment were the cornerstones of their relationship. They had chosen each other consistently through life's trials, building an unshakable foundation of trust over the years. Their commitment wasn't just about staying together but growing and evolving together, no matter their challenges.

Shared values and life goals had guided their journey. They had taken the time to align their core beliefs and aspirations, ensuring their path was purposeful and meaningful. Their shared values acted as a compass, providing direction and clarity in facing life's uncertainties.

Emotional and physical intimacy had remained vibrant in their relationship. They understood that sustaining emotional connection required open and honest communication, emotional support, and a willingness to be vulnerable. Physical intimacy was not neglected, as they prioritised this aspect of their partnership, understanding its significance in maintaining their bond.

Adapting to change had been a constant theme in their journey. They embraced life's transformations, facing personal and professional changes with resilience and understanding. They grew together, cherishing the lessons that came with each new chapter.

Both prioritised maintaining their individual identities. They encouraged each other's interests, friendships, and personal growth outside the relationship. This commitment to individuality enriched their partnership, allowing them to bring new experiences and perspectives to their lives together.

The art of conflict resolution had been mastered. They listened actively, empathised with each other's perspectives, and approached conflicts as opportunities for growth. Their conflicts strengthened their bond as they learned to navigate challenges as a team.

Continual investment in their relationship was non-negotiable. They regularly set aside time to connect, communicate, and express appreciation for each other. They never took their love for granted, always striving to keep the flame of their connection burning brightly.

Emily and Daniel's journey was a dance of lifelong love, a testament to the preparation and commitment required for an enduring partnership. Their story reminded us that a successful lifelong partnership requires depth, understanding, and ongoing effort. It was like a beautifully choreographed dance that evolved and matured over time, becoming more profound each year.

Do's and Don'ts

Do's:

1. **Build Trust and Commitment:** Consistently choose and prioritize each other, reinforcing the foundation of trust.

2. **Align on Values and Goals:** Discuss and align on core values and life goals to ensure mutual understanding and direction.

3. **Maintain Intimacy:** Keep both emotional and physical intimacy alive through continuous effort and connection.

4. **Adapt to Changes:** Embrace and adapt to life changes together, supporting each other through different stages.

5. **Preserve Individual Identities:** Encourage each other to maintain individual interests and friendships.

6. **Resolve Conflicts Effectively:** Develop healthy conflict resolution skills, focusing on empathy and understanding.

7. **Invest Continually in the Relationship:** Regularly dedicate time and effort to nurture and strengthen the relationship.

Don'ts:

1. **Neglect Trust-Building:** Avoid taking trust for granted; it requires ongoing effort and commitment.

2. **Ignore Value Misalignments:** Don't overlook differences in core values and goals, as they are crucial for long-term compatibility.

3. **Let Intimacy Wane:** Avoid neglecting emotional and physical intimacy; it needs regular nurturing.

4. **Resist Personal or Relationship Changes:** Don't be inflexible to changes in each other or the relationship dynamics.

5. **Overwhelm Individual Space:** Don't encroach on your partner's need for personal space and individuality.

6. **Avoid Addressing Conflicts:** Don't let conflicts go unresolved or approach them with a win-lose attitude.

7. **Complacency in Relationship Efforts:** Avoid becoming complacent; a lifelong partnership requires continuous nurturing and growth.

Starting Today
Embracing the Journey of Modern Love

Imagine standing on a busy street corner at twilight, watching the city lights flicker into view. Each glow represents a single story unfolding—some luminous with promise, others dimmed by disappointment. If you're someone who has navigated the dating world feeling invisible or disheartened, let this final chapter assure you that the insight you've gained from *Don't Date!* can guide you toward a more fulfilling path.

Reflecting on Personal Growth

Throughout this book, we've emphasized that modern dating is much more than a quest for companionship. It's also a journey of self-discovery. You've encountered the notion that relationships are mirrors, revealing both hidden strengths and vulnerabilities. With your new understanding, you won't be frightened by those reflections. Instead, you'll recognize them as milestones marking your evolution—opportunities to refine who you are and what you need.

From Heartbreak to Resilience

Heartbreak and rejection can sometimes feel like the weightiest chapters in your personal history. Perhaps you've wondered if all that time was wasted—chasing fleeting connections, repeating patterns that led nowhere. Yet, as we've explored, those moments can also spark resilience. Disappointment teaches you how to identify red flags early, how to assert your boundaries, and how to trust your instincts. Having read *Don't Date!*, you now have a framework for avoiding short-term entanglements that fail to appreciate your worth.

Navigating Complexity in Modern Dating

The world we date in today is undeniably complex. Apps and social media offer endless possibilities, yet they can also turn meaningful connections into fleeting encounters. Social norms around marriage, monogamy, and gender roles have shifted, leaving many of us uncertain about where we fit. This can be especially frustrating if you're a single woman who has seen more false starts than genuine beginnings.

But there is good news: you're no longer the same person who felt adrift in a sea of digital profiles. You've gained new perspectives on how technology can be harnessed to your advantage—or respectfully set aside when it creates more noise than clarity. By understanding these modern dynamics, you can recognize potential pitfalls and capitalize on genuine opportunities for real intimacy.

Cultivating Emotional Maturity and Self-Understanding

One key takeaway from *Don't Date!* is that emotional maturity underpins every lasting relationship. By exploring your own triggers, communicating assertively, and recognizing patterns in your behaviour, you've developed a deeper sense of self-awareness. This newly honed emotional intelligence will serve as your compass, guiding you toward partners who value open dialogue, mutual respect, and shared aspirations.

The Identity-Shaping Power of Relationships

Every relationship—whether it burns bright and short or stands the test of time—shapes our identity. When you understand how your past connections have influenced your beliefs and behaviour, you become empowered to decide what belongs in your future. No longer do you have to fit yourself into someone else's narrative. Instead, you can author your own story, choosing partners who support and inspire you.

Gratitude for the Road Travelled

It's natural to look back on your dating history and wish you'd avoided certain detours. But the frustrations and near-misses were never truly wasted. Each chapter played a part in clarifying who you are and what you can contribute to a relationship. Rather than dwelling on regret, *Don't Date!* encourages you to find gratitude for the lessons learned — lessons that have made you more discerning and, ultimately, more confident.

Choosing Your Next Steps

So here you stand at a new kind of threshold. Having read *Don't Date!*, you're equipped with sharper intuition, clearer boundaries, and a deeper understanding of how long-lasting relationships form. You know how to spot genuine compatibility and when to walk away from superficial entanglements. You recognize the importance of focusing on dynamics that foster trust, respect, and emotional safety.

Still, real life won't always unfold in predictable ways. You may encounter challenges or temptations to settle for less than you deserve. The difference now is that you're prepared. You've done the reflection and cultivated the emotional tools to make decisions that honor your worth.

A Future Shaped by Intentional Choices

Looking out at those city lights again, remember that each one—just like every new acquaintance—offers a possibility. But you no longer have to hope blindly that someone else will recognize your value. You realise it yourself. Empowered by the insights from *Don't Date!*, you can step forward with the confidence that your time, energy, and heart are worth investing in connections that genuinely resonate.

From this moment on, let your frustrations of the past serve as the fuel that propels you toward meaningful experiences. You stand poised and ready, with both knowledge and courage in hand. Yes, the future may still be filled with twists and turns, but you have the clarity to distinguish what is fleeting from what is worth nurturing. You have everything you need to shape a new direction in modern love—one where you make choices grounded in self-awareness, mutual respect, and genuine promise. And that, dear reader, is where your journey truly begins.

ooo

ABOUT THE AUTHOR

Hani Iskander has always been intrigued by systems—how they operate, why they falter, and what allows them to flourish. This lifelong curiosity guided him into the world of technology, where he spent years immersed in its rapid evolution. Later, he ventured into the intricate investment banking sector, embracing the challenge of understanding financial systems.

His journey took an unexpected turn before the dot-com bubble burst when Hani became an early investor in an internet dating platform. This gave him a front-row seat to the chaotic beginnings of digital matchmaking. At the same time, his experiences navigating the dating world provided valuable insights into the triumphs and struggles of finding meaningful connections in a fast-changing landscape.

Over the years, Hani listened to friends, colleagues, and acquaintances share their dating frustrations—stories of endless swiping, fleeting encounters, and difficulty finding genuine relationships. He noticed something surprising: these stories followed universal patterns despite their uniqueness. This sparked the idea for *Don't Date!*—a book that connects the dots, sheds light on the bigger picture, and offers a practical guide to navigating modern relationships.

Hani lives in Australia, balancing his passion for big ideas with his knack for simplifying life's complexities. Though he is not a psychologist or relationship expert, his keen observations and analytical approach provide fresh, relatable insights into the often-perplexing world of dating. Through humor and honesty, Hani aims to make the journey toward lasting love more understandable—and maybe even enjoyable.

www.ingramcontent.com/pod-product-compliance
Lightning Source LLC
Chambersburg PA
CBHW022336280326
41934CB00006B/661